HERO STREET, U.S.A.

The Hero Street monument. Photo by Marc Wilson.

HERO STREET, U.S.A.

The Story of Little Mexico's Fallen Soldiers

Marc Wilson

UNIVERSITY OF OKLAHOMA PRESS : NORMAN

All photos are courtesy of Joe Terronez unless otherwise indicated.

Library of Congress Cataloging-in-Publication Data
Wilson, Marc, 1951–
    Hero Street, U.S.A. : the story of Little Mexico's fallen soldiers / Marc Wilson.
    p. cm.
    Includes bibliographical references and index.
    ISBN 978-0-8061-4012-4 (hardcover : alk. paper) 1. Mexican American soldiers — Illinois — Silvis — History — 20th century. 2. Veterans — Illinois — Silvis — History — 20th century. 3. Silvis (Ill.) — History, Military — 20th century. 4. World War, 1939–1945 — Participation, Mexican American. 5. Mexican American soldiers — Illinois — Silvis — Biography. 6. Heroes — Illinois — Silvis — Biography. 7. Mexican Americans — Illinois — Silvis — Social conditions — 20th century. 8. Mexican American neighborhoods — Illinois — Silvis — History — 20th century. 9. Silvis (Ill.) — Biography. 10. Silvis (Ill.) — Ethnic relations — History — 20th century. I. Title.
    F549.S55W55 2009
    940.54′6773 — dc22   2008035613

The paper in this book meets the guidelines for permanence and durability of the committee on Production Guidelines for Book Longevity of the Council on Library Resources, Inc. ∞

Copyright © 2009 by Marc Wilson. Published by the University of Oklahoma Press, Norman, Publishing Division of the University. Manufactured in the U.S.A.

1 2 3 4 5 6 7 8 9 10

To Ginny,
with love, always

Contents

List of Illustrations	ix
Preface	xi
Prologue	3
1. Angelina's Anguish	9
2. Wedding and Revolution	13
3. The Devil's Highway	21
4. Red Boxcar	29
5. No Man's Land, Again	38
6. Odd Child Out	45
7. New Suit for Graduation	54
8. One Family per Stall	64
9. Little Hands	81
10. Boy with the Borrowed, Misspelled Name	93
11. The Last Battle	107
12. Bunker Hill, Korea	119
13. Last to Die	133
14. Homecomings	141
15. Blackballed	148

16. Thank God, Paved at Last   152
Epilogue   163

Notes   167
Bibliography   179
Index   185

Illustrations

The Hero Street monument   *Frontispiece*
Louis Ramirez and his wife, Mary   4
St. Mary of Guadaloupe Catholic Church, Romita, Mexico   15
Eduviges and Angelina Sandoval and family   34
Boxcar church in Silvis, Illinios   36
Tony Pompa   50
Frank Sandoval   56
Willie Sandoval   69
Claro Solis   83
Peter Masias   95
Joseph Sandoval   109
Joseph Gomez   121
Johnny Muños   138
The Sandoval house   144
Jesse Perez, Lt. Col. D. H. McClinton, Vicente Ximenes,
      and Joe Terronez   160

Preface

Until December 7, 1941, the people of Little Mexico in Silvis, Illinois, rarely traveled far from their homes. Their jobs, schools, friends, stores, taverns, church, and cemetery were, by necessity, within walking distance. Families were large and poor, and, as the Great Depression dragged on, they spent few dollars beyond necessities. The old people — those who had fled to the United States during the Mexican Revolution — lived pretty much as they had back in Mexico, speaking Spanish, working hard, and loving their children, their church, and their neighbors. They aspired mainly to survive — to feed and house their children, and perhaps send a few dollars back to family members in Mexico. Their children spoke English and Spanish, went to school, and aspired to be Americans, but saw few opportunities — until the Japanese attacked Pearl Harbor. Then, America needed them, and the young men of Little Mexico responded. They'd finally found a way to escape the bottom rung of society — where their kind had been stuck since time immemorial.

When the United States entered World War II, the young men of Little Mexico volunteered en masse for military service. In that war and in the Korean conflict that followed, seventy-eight men from some thirty-five houses on 2nd Street served in the military. They saw military service as a chance to prove themselves patriotic Americans. One of the men, Claro Solis, said he hoped he could "win a gold star for mother" — an honor reserved for families of men killed in action. Solis' mother received a star — one of six sent to unpaved 2nd Street during World War II. Two more men from 2nd Street earned gold stars in the Korean War. The eight combat deaths are most likely the most from any single block in America.

Mexican American soldiers and sailors found equality in military service. One historian said that, for Mexican Americans, the experience of the war years marked "the first time they were participating fully in mainstream society, even working alongside Anglos as equals." Unlike African Americans, Latinos weren't segregated by the military during World War II. Solis wrote home from boot camp that his officers "treated him like a white man." Another Mexican American soldier said, "When the war started, I became a white man."

Equality had limits. Those who saw combat "represented a distinct minority among the millions of soldiers in the U.S. Army in World War II." The U.S. Defense Department estimates that between four hundred thousand and five hundred thousand Latinos served in World War II. The army assigned soldiers to duties based largely on their Army General Classification Test, which was "somewhat biased against those without the benefits of extensive education, travel or experience." That description fit the soldiers from 2nd Street in Silvis. As always, there was dirty work to do, and the men from 2nd Street got some of the worst assignments, at the front lines. They were used to it. When their parents fled to the United States, they worked the worst jobs and lived in and raised their children in old boxcars because the whites wouldn't let them reside in town. So it wasn't surprising that war meant combat duty in foxholes at the front.

President John F. Kennedy, in a June 19, 1963, speech to Congress, said, "No one has been barred on account of his race from fighting or dying for America." In fact, race likely added to the chances that the men from 2nd Street were killed in action. When they finally left Little Mexico, the men of 2nd Street traveled and fought in Africa, the Pacific, Asia, and Europe. They died on the other side of the world in Burma, Italy, Belgium, the Netherlands, Germany, and Korea. The survivors on 2nd Street—now Hero Street, U.S.A.—don't begrudge ultimate sacrifices paid by their sons, husbands, fathers, and brothers. They wear the men's deaths as tear-stained badges of honor. The survivors—the returning soldiers and sailors, and the family and friends of the eight who didn't return home—ask only for acknowledgement of their part in American history. I hope this book helps give that.

I first heard of Hero Street, U.S.A. just after I was appointed to the editorial board of the *Quad City Times*, which has a circulation area that includes Silvis. Although Hero Street was widely known in the Quad Cities, as a newcomer to the area, I suspected that it had received little national attention. Area newspapers had reported about Hero Street, but much of the coverage was shallow and dealt with narrow, bitter disputes about how best to erect a monument at Hero Street. The bigger picture wasn't widely understood.

Local residents honor Hero Street every Memorial Day and Veterans Day with parades, flags, and speeches, but I found to my amazement that even keynote speakers didn't quite know their facts, even mixing up the dates and locations of the heroes' deaths. The web sites that promoted Hero Street were slim on details, and requests posted for biographical information about the lives of the eight heroes weren't answered. It seemed to me that the in-depth story of Hero Street, U.S.A. was being lost to history. More generally, I agree with Professor Maggie Rivas-Rodriquez of the University of Texas, who noted: "General treatments of World War II, of the great Depression, and the postwar years in America generally exclude stories of U.S. Latinos, as if Latinos had not lived here, had not served the country, had not, as a matter of fact, made the ultimate sacrifice." So I began digging, reading, and interviewing. The research was one of the great experiences of my life.

Many of the family members of the eight heroes maintain scrapbooks, and preserve their letters, medals, and ribbons. Almost all family members — mostly younger brothers and sisters, cousins — and friends eagerly cooperated with me. They want the story of Hero Street, U.S.A. told. Their stories and quotes — based on hours of interviews and access to letters and memorabilia — are at the heart of this story. To help ensure accuracy, I asked at least one family member to read the chapter about their loved one. I chose not to footnote each interview I conducted, but instead I reserved footnotes for the extensive secondary sources I used to help tell this story.

Hero Street residents, family members of the Heroes, Silvis city officials, at least one member of Congress, and the Illinois Legislature claim that the eight men from 2nd Street in Silvis are the "most of any one street in America killed in combat." The claim has been read into in the Congressional Record, and in regional newspapers and national magazines, on videos and television shows, and over the Internet. But there is no official block-by-block count of combat fatalities — at least not that I could find. Former Silvis Mayor Joe Terronez, who has done as much as anyone to honor the heroes, told me: "We've said Hero Street, U.S.A. has the most combat deaths on any block — and it has been reported all over — for many years, and no one has disputed it." Other towns deserve honors — Brooklyn, NY, likely sent the most soldiers per capita into World War II. One family — the Sullivans of Waterloo, Iowa — lost five sons who were aboard the USS *Juneau* when it was sunk on November 13, 1942.

So I can't prove — though I believe it to be true — that Hero Street suffered the most combat deaths of any single block in America. But even if the claim is disputable, the tale of the eight Heroes, their families' exodus from Mexico, and their battle to survive in America is fascinating — at least to the author, and, I hope, to the reader.

My wife, Ginny, and I also made two trips to the state of Guanajuato, Mexico, to better understand the roots of this story. We visited the churches and hometowns of the parents of the eight heroes. When I think of Hero Street, U.S.A., I regard the people who fled Mexico for the United States as heroes. I think the exodus of Mexicans during the Mexican Revolution as another untold story of bravery and heroism. The fleeing Mexicans rarely shared the horrors of the revolution with their children, many of whom said they learned much about their parents and siblings through my research.

As a guide to readers, I note that this book is divided roughly into three sections. The first tells the story of the exodus of peons and peasants from Mexico to Silvis, and the lives of the Mexicans before and during the Great Depression. World War II marks the beginning of the second section, which profiles each of the eight men from Hero Street who died in action. Each hero is given a chapter. I ordered the chapters chronologically by the dates of their deaths, beginning with Tony Pompa in Italy in January 1943 and ending with Johnny Muños's death in Korea in August 1951. The third section, starting with chapter 14, talks about the aftermath of the wars, and the discrimination that returning Latino veterans faced back in the United States. The grace — and, in fact, the seeming lack of anger — shown by the returning veterans deeply impressed me, as did their dogged determination to gain full and equal status as U.S. citizens.

In addition to interviews with family members and friends, I relied heavily on many historians to tell the story of the battles that claimed the heroes' lives. Videos produced by WGN TV and Busch Creative Services also captured the story of Hero Street residents who died before I became interested in the story. Former Silvis Mayor Joe Terronez, one of Hero Street's strongest advocates, made hundreds of records easily accessible to me. Frank Soliz of the Hero Street Monument Committee also was exceptionally generous at all turns.

My number one source was Tanilo "Tony" Sandoval, who was tireless and patient in helping me sort out the story of his parents, Eduviges and Angelina Sandoval, and his two brothers, heroes Joe and Frank Sandoval. He knows where all the bodies are buried, and he guards their memories and their graves with great care and love.

My friend Jack Quick read each version of every re-written chapter with great enthusiasm. The University of Oklahoma Press greatly helped me with this, my first, book; I offer special kudos to Editor-in-Chief Charles Rankin, acquisitions editor Matt Bokovoy, and manuscript editor Julie Shilling. Freelance copyeditor Steven Weingarten was a joy to work with. Galen Schroeder was passionate in his fine efforts to create the index.

I tried to remain true to history, but I'm sure much may have been lost over time, in the fog of war, in the faded memories of my sources, and in errors and mistakes I inadvertently made. Most of all, I thank my wife, Ginny, for her unending patience, copyediting, critiques, and willingness to help me pursue research about Hero Street, U.S.A.

Marc Wilson
June 23, 2008
Hampton, IL

HERO STREET, U.S.A.

Prologue

Loved and tender son,
This is the will of the gods.
You are not born in your true house
Because you are a warrior. Your land
Is not here, but in another place.
You are promised to the field of battle.
You are dedicated to war.
You must give the Sun your enemies' blood.
You must feed the earth with corpses.
Your house, your fortune, and your destiny
Is in the House of the Sun.
Serve, and rejoice that you may be worthy
To die the Death of Flowers!
— From "The Prayer of the Mexican Midwife"

The eighty-seven-year-old man sat in his wheelchair on his home's elevated side porch overlooking the Hero Street, U.S.A. monument in Silvis, Illinois. A bright near-noon September sun heated the breezeless Saturday, but the old man wore a heavy

Louis Ramirez and his wife, Mary, the sister of Johnny Muños, watch from their home as part of the Hero Street monument is delivered to Hero Street Park, May 2004. Photo by Jeff Cook, courtesy of the *Quad-City Times*.

sweater, and a folded blanket rested on his lap. Alzheimer's Disease devoured his recent memories, but he remembered, as though it was yesterday, his childhood friends whose unblinking bronze faces peered from the war memorial. Few remember the eight heroes as living flesh and bone, but the old man did. With a wave, he welcomed a stranger. "I am Louis Ramirez. I have lived here many, many years." He pointed at the monument. "They were my friends. I don't remember well now, except for what happened a long time ago. I remember *mi compadres* — my brothers."

Louis remembered everyone going to war. "We were all very patriotic. We all wanted to be Americans and fight for our country. Nobody knows how patriotic we Mexican Americans were." Nearly eighty men from the street served in World War II and Korea. After the Japanese struck Pearl Harbor on December 7, 1941, "the residents of . . . 2nd Street in Silvis, Illinois, now called Hero Street, contributed more men to the armed forces . . . than any other area of its size in the country," said a Resolution approved by the Illinois House of Representatives on October 26, 1971. The story of Hero Street, the resolution added, is "a lesson in perfect, unselfish patriotism." Representative Lane Evans (D-Illinois), read a similar statement into the Congressional Record on November 18, 1983. Evans's resolution says more men from 2nd Street died in battle for the United States than from any other single block in America. From thirty-five tiny houses, shacks and old boxcars turned into houses came seventy-eight soldiers and sailors.

Immediately after Pearl Harbor, Louis joined the U.S. Army, which assigned him to the 132nd Infantry Regiment of the Illinois National Guard. His unit went to New Caledonia where it became part of the new Americal Division. His unit arrived on Guadalcanal on December 8, 1942. Some thirty thousand Japanese soldiers and sailors died in the battle, while eight thousand American soldiers, sailors and marines died. "Yes, I remember Guadalcanal, but I don't talk about it and I don't want to think about it," Louis said. He preferred to talk about his friends, now just faces on the war memorial.

When he returned home from World War II, he found that six of his friends — Tony Pompa, Frank Sandoval, Willie Sandoval, Claro Solis, Peter Masias and Joe Sandoval — hadn't survived. "Understand — we didn't have money or cars or clothes — and our parents didn't have anything either. All we had was each other, our friends and our family. We could go into any house and get something to eat. We were all one big family. We didn't have nothing, but we had each other. These boys were my brothers. We all worked out at the punching bag, and we played football on Sundays and baseball in the summer. We used the street to sled on when it snowed. We all had caves in the big hill. We stuck together at school. At night, we all climbed to the top of the hill and built big fires, and we drank beer when we could get any. And we sang old Mexican songs.

"Peter Masias," Louis said, "lived right across the street, over there. He had the best voice. He could really sing. He never owned a guitar. His family was really poor. Peter was a good boy. He got killed on a [parachute] drop in Germany." The old man pointed across the street again, down several houses to the south. "Peter ate most of the time at the Pompa's. One of his best friends was Tony Pompa. Tony really liked the girls, and the girls really liked him — they say he was movie-star handsome."

Did he know Angelina and Eduviges Sandoval, and their sons Joe and Frank? "Of course, I remember them. Joe was real smart and a real good baseball player and he got married and had two sons before he got drafted and killed real late in the war. Joe was about my age. And Frank, he was a good boy, real hard working. Real quiet, too. He got it in Burma."

Claro Solis, Louis said, "wanted to be an artist, and he thought he was going to be something. He was real serious in school and very religious. He wanted to be somebody special. His sister's husband died, and he spent a lot of time with his sister and her daughters — almost like their father. He was a real good guy. He got it in the Battle of the Bulge."

Willie Sandoval's face also peers out of the monument. "He was *mi compadre*, too," Louis said. "He was really a tough guy. But a real nice guy. He and his brother Reuben were boxers. They had to keep their weight down all the time. Even when there was food, they didn't eat much. But there usually wasn't much food in that house." He laughed and said, "All of us from 2nd Street probably gained weight when we went into the service — that was the first time we got all the food we could eat."

Two more faces peer out from the war memorial — Joe Gomez and Johnny Muños. Although they were younger, Louis remembers them, too. "They were younger and hung out with other kids, but I knew them. They got killed in Korea, you know. My wife is Johnny's sister. And Joe Gomez was really brave. He got the Silver Star, but he probably should have gotten the Medal of Honor." Louis said it would be good "to write everything down so people will remember — remember how we volunteered and fought and died for our country, and how much we love this country. Mexicans are good fighters and good Americans."

In 1969, city and U.S. postal officials formally designated 2nd Street in Silvis, Illinois, "Hero Street, U.S.A." In a nutshell, the story is this: In a fifteen-month period ending in April 1945 six men from this one unpaved street in Western Illinois were killed in action in World War II. Two more men from the same block were killed in action in the Korean War. That may be the most killed in war from any one block in the United States. But the story runs even deeper. The parents of the eight men on the memorial also have their names carved in granite. They fled to the United States during the Mexican Revolution, seeking mere survival for themselves, and hope for something greater for their children and grandchildren. They lived in boxcars and performed some of the dirtiest work in the nation. They faced a never-ending threat of being sent back to Mexico. They lived without the rights of citizenship and came from a country unable to do much for their citizens. In the Great Depression, millions suffered — but few were poorer than the hundreds of people who lived in Silvis' Little Mexico. Their sons were among the first to offer their lives to defend America — and to prove that the United States was their country. The story of Hero Street is largely untold, and U.S. history is incomplete without this story.

Mexico is present within the United States, and to understand the United States, one needs to understand Mexico. "Our countries are neighbors, condemned to live alongside each other," wrote the Mexican poet Octavio Paz. "They are separated, however, more by profound social, economic, and psychic differences than by physical and political frontiers." Before the Mexican Revolution, Mexican immigration into the United States had been "minuscule" — just 103,393 reported in 1900. In 1910, the U.S. Census reported 221,915 descendants of the citizens who'd lived in the territory — Texas, California, Nevada, Utah, New Mexico, Arizona, and parts of Colorado and Wyoming — that had been part of Mexico before the Mexican-American War. Then came the Mexican Revolution, and 890,371 immigrants fled from Mexico to the United States between 1910 and 1920. "The war [in Mexico] brought an end to everything. . . . Life was very sad," said one Mexican who fled to the United States. Many Mexicans found jobs working for the United States' six largest railroads, including the Chicago, Rock Island and Pacific Railroad in Silvis. The Rock Island, as it was commonly called, gave Mexican refugees homes — forty to sixty red boxcars (the number varied over time) in the nine hundred-acre Silvis rail yard. In those boxcars, hundreds of American children were born to Mexican parents. From this "Little Mexico," eight boys became American heroes — killed in action, fighting for their country.

History celebrates mostly the rich and powerful, those who leave diaries and letters and newspaper clippings. Biographies are written about presidents, potentates, kings and generals — rarely peons, illiterates, aliens, and foot soldiers. The heroes in this story kept no diaries, wrote few letters and went mostly unreported by newspapers — so something happened in America that went largely unnoticed. Yet today, one in seven Americans is Hispanic — a number that is growing. Hispanics are increasingly prosperous and influential in the United States. More can be told to explain how this happened. "Mexican Americans," Louis Ramirez says from his wheelchair, "are willing to fight and die for this country. It is our country now, too. People should understand us and know of our sacrifices. We gave our blood to be Americans. We are part of this country."

CHAPTER ONE

Angelina's Anguish

Do we truly live on earth?
Not forever here,
Only a little while.
Even jade breaks,
Golden things fall apart,
Precious feathers fade;
Not forever on earth,
Only a moment here.
— Mexica poet Nezahualcoyotl[1]

The boy on the bicycle knew the route too well. He left the Western Union office in downtown Moline, Illinois, and rode northeast along the Mississippi River. He pedaled along 4th Avenue in Moline, then down 16th Avenue in East Moline. Entering the railroad town of Silvis, Illinois, he pedaled a short distance along 1st Avenue before turning right onto 2nd Street in the neighborhood known as "Little Mexico." It was the poorest part of town, and the condition of the street, unpaved and soaked by recent rain showers, forced the messenger to dismount and push his bicycle through clinging mud in order to reach his destination.

The date was May 8, 1945: VE (Victory in Europe) Day for the Western Allies. Nazi Germany had formally surrendered, ending World War II in Europe, and joyful Americans throughout the land were taking to the streets in spontaneous outpourings of joy and celebration. But there could be little rejoicing that day on 2nd Street in Silvis — not with the boy on the bicycle delivering "regrets from the Secretary of War" — for the sixth time since the conflict began. Already five framed golden stars hung from the front windows of the neighborhood's tiny houses — one that was little more than a shack, some mere boxcars. The messenger passed on his right the little house at 124 2nd Street, home of the Masias family, where he had stopped a few weeks earlier after Peter Masias had parachuted into heavy antiaircraft fire east of the Elbe River. He passed the tiny, one-story home at 146 2nd Street, also on his right, where a star honored Claro Solis' sacrifice in the Battle of the Bulge; and he went by the house at 182 2nd Street, home of the Pompa family, the first in Little Mexico to receive a visit from the boy on the bicycle after Tony Pompa's bomber was shot down over Italy in January 1944. The messenger pushed on, passing on his left a steep hill pocked with caves, a natural playground for a group of boys — that probably included Joe Gomez and Johnny Muños. In the next war, telegrams would be delivered to their families at 144 2nd Street and 181 2nd Street. Next, on the right side at 214 2nd Street, stood Willie Sandoval's house, which the messenger visited after the Allies tried to capture one bridge too many in Holland.

Six telegrams came within a fifteen-month period, and residents in the thirty houses that lined the street watched each time as the telegrams were delivered. The block had sent seventy-eight men to war after Pearl Harbor. They were the residents' sons, brothers, fathers, godsons, friends, and lovers. They had shared most everything — mothers had even nursed others' sons. Children trailed the boy as he pushed his bike up the road. Adults followed him with their eyes and prayers. Old Mexican women fingered their rosaries, praying continuously in Spanish. "Hail Mary, full of grace. The Lord is with thee . . . at the hour of our death, amen. Hail Mary, full of grace. The Lord is with thee . . . at the hour of our death, amen."

On this day, the young messenger stopped in front of the little two-story wood-frame house at 187 2nd Street, the home of Eduviges and Angelina Sandoval and their ten children, daughter-in-law, and two grandsons. A framed gold star already hung from the window. The messenger leaned his bike against the hill, climbed thirteen worn wooden steps to the house, and knocked on the front door. Without uttering a word — he knew no Spanish, those within little English — the boy passed the telegram inside. Angelina Sandoval read no English — in fact she read no language — but when she saw the boy at her front door she needed no translation. She read death in the boy's presence, and she spoke the language of anguish. Her sobbing began before anyone read the telegram. The army sent the telegram to Nellie Sandoval, Angelina's daughter-in-law. "The Secretary of War desires me to express his deep regret that your husband, Private First Class Joseph Sandoval, was reported missing in action on April 14, 1945 in Germany."

The boy on the bike had brought an almost identical telegram in the summer of 1944: "The Secretary of War desires me to express his deep regret that your son, Private First Class Frank Sandoval, was killed in action on 26 June, 1944, in North Burma." Nellie cried and hugged her two baby boys, Mike and Henry. Always stoic in public, Eduviges said little, but now he also hugged his family. Angelina broke into sobs heard in every house on the street. Some say her sobs still haunt the neighborhood. "Missing, mama, Joe's only missing!" said her daughter, Georgia. But Angelina knew better — she knew death too well: death in Mexico, death up and down the street, death again in her home. She was right — Joe never would come home, expect in a coffin. "It was very sad for me when they told me my son was going to leave for war," Angelina told a reporter through a translator many years after Joe died. "And I still feel sad about it."

After delivering the telegram the Western Union boy simply turned around, descended the thirteen steps, got his bike, and rode off. There was no ceremony. "You see in the movies where they send officers in dress uniforms and big cars with flags to break the news, but that wasn't how it was back then for us," said Tanilo Sandoval, younger brother of Joe and Frank Sandoval. "They just sent young boys on bikes with form telegrams. When you saw them riding down your street you knew something terrible had happened. We saw the boy on the bike way too often."

CHAPTER TWO

Wedding and Revolution

Mucho trabajo,
Poco dinero,
No hay frijoles;
Viva Madero!
— Popular Mexican rhyme

Each Sunday morning, no matter how late he came home the night before or how badly his head throbbed, Eduviges Sandoval rose from bed first to wake his family to get ready for 7:00 A.M. mass. He slipped his feet into heavy work boots and wrapped himself in his long, oft-patched coat. He pushed the front door open, went outside, and climbed down the exterior wooden stairway that was the lone route to the basement where his wife and four daughters slept on homemade beds and mats. If it was cold, he threw a sawed-off chunk of a railroad tie into the wood-burning stove, stirred the ashes; then he woke his wife and daughters with kisses and calls of "buenos dias, mi niñas." Then he climbed back upstairs, touched the switch, and light and memories flooded the room. Sons Joe and Frank, tired of living like poor Mexicans, had brought electric power to the house, wiring switches and hooking up lights. Now he had light, but not Joe and

13

Frank. The light and his voice rousted his other sons. The boys had to go to mass too. But not Eduviges—he crawled back into bed. Sleep, he figured, would cure his hangover better than God could repair his battered soul.

Eduviges drank too much. Prohibition ended in 1933, and when the taverns reopened in the depths of the Great Depression, he became a regular at the nearby bars that catered to Mexican railroad workers. The drinking didn't affect his job performance, and he never missed a day of work. He worked the worst hours in the worst conditions, and never sought promotions. He never argued with the bosses. He tipped his hat to everyone, and insisted his children to do likewise. He paid his taxes on time and dutifully registered as a foreign alien with the U.S. government every January—even after the government had taken his sons and not returned them. He declined to sign protest petitions asking the city to pave 2nd Street. He made sure his children and grandsons had food and clothes and went to school. Part of his meager paycheck went to the church, and he prided himself on being the first one up on Sunday mornings to get his family ready for mass. But then he went back to bed. No longer could he genuflect before the crucifix. He no longer believed in God or the church. It was his lone protest.

Eduviges once believed in God, the Pope in Rome, the priests and the church. He was baptized into the Roman Catholic Church, his mother recited the rosary every night while he went to sleep, and a priest taught him to read from the Holy Bible. He and Angelina were married in a beautiful sixteenth century Roman Catholic Church in Romita, Mexico's "Little Rome." That day may have been the high point—and the beginning of the end—of Eduviges' faith. That day he believed in two messiahs—Jesus Christ of Nazareth and Francisco Madero of Coahuila. Eduviges and Angelina married on June 3, 1911, the same day Madero—the new "savior of Mexico" and the "Apostle of Democracy"—began his tour of the country while en route to Mexico City. Madero triggered the revolution that forced the ouster of dictator Porfirio Díaz after thirty-eight years in power. On Eduviges' and Angelina's wedding day, peasants and peons celebrated—and sometimes rioted—in honor

St. Mary of Guadaloupe Catholic Church, where Eduviges and Angelina Sandoval were married in June 1914, Romita, Mexico. Photo by Marc Wilson.

of Madero's ascension and Díaz's ouster. In nearby Leon, some three hundred rioters broke into the massive municipal building off the Plaza Central and robbed the city coffers. Rioting occurred in nearby Ceyala and in San Miguel de Allende. In cities, towns, and villages across Mexico, bands of gun-toting men looted business, banks, and government buildings, and broke down prison doors and freed political and criminal inmates. Occasionally, they tortured and even killed followers of Díaz. Most Mexicans, most of them poor, celebrated that day — a seemingly auspicious start to the married life of Eduviges and Angelina.

Angelina was just fourteen on her wedding day, and had rarely left her family's tiny adobe home. She was born August 30, 1896, to Silbiano and Ramona Hernandez. She was illiterate — as were 95 percent of Mexico's peasant/peon class of women. She barely knew Eduviges, who was ten years older and a tall, mustachioed, handsome, cowboy hat–wearing, weather-beaten peon/vaquero who worked on the vast Hacienda Rana, named for the region's croaking frogs. By Mexican Catholic tradition, Angelina and Eduviges probably had met only under carefully chaperoned situations. Their conversations would have been limited to *dichos*— trite, meaningless expressions. She knew little of Mexico's affairs — that, for instance, real wages were lower for most Mexicans than they had been a century earlier when the Spanish were finally driven out of Mexico after a three hundred-year reign; that while the elite prospered, an appallingly high infant and early childhood mortality rate (40 percent of children died before age five) reduced to just thirty years the average life span of the vast majority of Mexicans. As peons, Eduviges and Angelina were virtual slaves on the foreign-owned hacienda, where "exploitation had deep, centuries-old roots and entailed the lifelong and hereditary serfdom of laborers forever in debt to their 'masters.' " Some three thousand families owned almost half of the land in Mexico, and just seventeen individuals owned one-fifth of the country. Nearly 15 million Mexicans worked for a handful of masters, including many foreigners.

Madero, a wealthy spiritualist who sought guidance from the dead, ran against Díaz in the 1910 election, arguing that Mexico's constitution limited presidents to one term. After rigged results gave Díaz an eighth term (and Madero only 196 votes), Madero denounced the election as fraudulent and called for a nationwide uprising to begin November 20, 1910. In response, men across the country took to arms and began the Mexican Revolution, a prolonged and violent upheaval that would ultimately claim some one million lives. Madero's forces won battles in the north and south of Mexico and, on May 21, 1911, Díaz resigned and went into exile. Peons and peasants hailed Madero as their political messiah: finally, they hoped, there would be land and justice for everyone — not for just the very rich, the very few. But Madero didn't comprehend the urgency of the peoples' desire for sweeping social and economic change. "Almost immediately," wrote one historian, "he was beset by conspiracies and open opposition; even those who fought for him turned against him."

As Madero took power in Mexico City, the newlyweds moved in with Eduviges' parents, younger brother, and three sisters, probably all living in a small mud-and-adobe home with no electricity or running water. They lived lifestyles that hadn't changed much since Cortés conquered Mexico and established "New Spain" almost four hundred years earlier. The Sandovals worked long, grueling days, and slept in hammocks or on mats on a dirt floor. The quality of life on the hacienda was "miserable and hopeless: filthy, overcrowded huts, an unbalanced meager diet, ever-constant death, disability and disease. . . . Few, if any schools were available to hacienda children, and the survivors of infancy had little to look forward to but their parents' misery. The average peon . . . remained eternally in debt, either to his patron or to the hacienda store. Owners "bought and sold each other's peon[s] and used bounty hunters to track down fugitives, who would then be beaten to death as a bloody warning to the others."

Angelina labored as Mexican women had for centuries, drawing water from deep wells, hand scrubbing clothes, grinding corn, preserving vegetables, and hauling food to ranch hands in the far-flung cane fields and livestock pastures. Eduviges' wage was equivalent to between twelve and eighteen cents a day. He also received a ration of corn. Angelina was paid about half that. Writer Luis Alberto Urrea described life on a hacienda: "The People had never seen paved streets, street lamps, a trolley, or a ship. Steps were an innovation that seemed an occult work, stairways were the wicked cousins of ladders, and greatly to be avoided. Even the streets of [neighboring villages], trod on certain Sundays when the People formed a long parade and left the safety of the hacienda to attend mass, were dirt, or cobble, not paved. The People thought all great cities had pigs in the streets and great muddy rivers of mule piss attracting hysterical swarms of wasps, and that all places were built of dirt and straw."

They lived in poverty, but in peace until the generals and the American ambassador turned on the messiah Madero, and started civil war.

In the cold, damp pre-dawn hours of Sunday, February 9, 1913, seven hundred Mexican soldiers arrived in Mexico City after an all-night forced march. Oxen and mules pulled cannon and Gatling Guns. The soldiers, led by twenty-two mutinous generals, marched to the Santiago Tlatelolco Prison and at gunpoint freed Gen. Bernardo Reyes and Felix Díaz, nephew of the deposed dictator. The mutineers' plan called for Reyes to address the nation and declare himself president of Mexico. But Reyes was met by soldiers loyal to Madero, who fired machine guns, rifles, and mortars from the roof of the National Palace. In a ten-minute battle, Reyes and some four hundred others died. President Madero gave command of the Loyalist forces to Gen. Victoriano Huerta—one of the great misjudgments in Mexican history. For four days, as both sides fought a war of attrition, artillery barrages and infantry attacks caused at least five hundred casualties, including many civilians. As food became scarce, cats and dogs vanished.

The mutineers had a powerful friend in the American embassy, Ambassador Henry Lane Wilson, who disliked Madero because of his anti-American rhetoric and his attempts to tax Mexican oil pumped by foreign oil companies. Wilson told American newspapers that Madero was a communist, corrupt, and should be locked in a madhouse. Wilson wrote to Washington that the Mexican president was allowing American property to be confiscated "through legal methods which would be a disgrace to the civilization of the Middle Ages." Americans had much to lose — before Madero took power, Americans owned more than 40 percent of Mexico's land, mines, and oil industry, and other foreign nationals owned another 24 percent. On February 12, Wilson met with Díaz and his mutineers, and then publicly threatened intervention by the U.S. military, prompting some Mexican senators to urge Madero to resign. On February 16, Wilson wrote the German ambassador to Mexico that Huerta, Madero's top general, "has . . . been in secret negotiations with Díaz; he would come out openly against Madero if he were not afraid that the foreign powers would deny him recognition. . . . I have let him know that I am willing to recognize any government that is able to restore peace and order instead of Mr. Madero's government." In his own memoir, Wilson wrote that "(I) determined that I must take a decisive step on my own responsibility to bring about a restoration of order. . . . I decided to ask Generals Huerta and Díaz to come to the embassy." The three concluded the *Pacto de la Empanada* (Embassy Pact) under which Huerta would become interim president until Díaz could be "elected" president. On February 18, with Huerta's endorsement, soldiers swept into the National Palace and arrested Madero and Vice President Jose Maria Pino Suárez. Thirty minutes before Madero was arrested, Wilson wired Washington that the Mexican Army had taken control of the country. After Madero was arrested, Madero's wife went to the U.S. embassy to beg for Wilson's help. The American ambassador refused her, saying: "I will be frank with you, madam. Your husband's downfall is due to the fact that he never wanted to consult with me."

The next day, while Huerta attended a party celebrating George Washington's birthday at the U.S. embassy, soldiers escorted Madero out of the capital and shot him in the back of the head at point-blank range. Vice President Suárez was put in front of a penitentiary wall and shot to death by a firing squad. Huerta promptly appointed himself acting president of Mexico. A German diplomat wrote: "Ambassador Wilson planned the coup. He himself boasts of it." Wilson asked Washington to recognize Huerta's regime, but President William Howard Taft deferred the decision to incoming President Woodrow Wilson. The new president, shocked by Madero's murder, refused to recognize Huerta's government, and recalled Ambassador Wilson.

The assassination of Madero and his vice president is known in Mexico as the Decena Tragicia — Ten Tragic Days — and "all the central images are engraved in Mexican history." Their murders created martyrs and re-ignited the Mexican Revolution, turning most of Mexico into near anarchy, and parts of Mexico into Hell on Earth. The last great bloody battle of the revolution would be fought near the home of Eduviges and Angelina Sandoval. The toll in human lives was huge. Between 1910 and 1920, one out of fifteen Mexicans — one million people — lost their lives. And Eduviges Sandoval — his son believes — began to wonder: Had God forsaken Mexico? Did He even exist? Or was He just a God of Vengeance? So Eduviges stayed home every Sunday.

CHAPTER THREE

The Devil's Highway

It is said that in Mexico it is impossible to take a census. The birth rate is so high and the death rate so fantastic that only a rough approximation is at all possible.
— Victor Villaseñor

Drunken, celebrating soldiers rode their horses into Dolores Saucedo's general store in León, Mexico, in June 1915. They fired their rifles into the ceiling and walls, then took aim at Saucedo and accused him of selling goods to Pancho Villa's men. They found proof—Villa pesos in the cash register. "Senors, por favor! We had no choice but to take the money," Dolores told them. "They had guns. They would have killed us. Clemencia, por favor!"

Soldiers on all sides in the Mexican Revolution had devised many cruel punishments for traitors. Suspects could simply be shot on the spot, but there was little sport in that. They could be hanged by the neck, slowly strangling as a crowd watched and cheered. They could be dragged behind a horse until dead, and then some. Or they could be buried alive, or perhaps buried up to their necks so their captors could ride their horses over them. The question became: How would these soldiers dispose of the traitor Dolores Saucedo? The answer: Use the shovels he sold in his store.

One of the drunken soldiers grabbed a shovel and threw it at Saucedo, then marched him at gunpoint out of his store and into the street, and ordered him to dig his own grave. The soldiers made family, neighbors, and friends watch, and none dared intervene. Life was cheap, and death and torture common in those days, especially that day, the day the once seemingly invincible Pancho Villa lost his last great battle. Some in the crowd—Villa supporters yesterday, Obregón men today—jeered Saucedo for being a rich merchant who'd traded with the losing side; others mocked and taunted him and called for him to dig faster. Saucedo wept and pleaded for his life. He swore that he was no traitor, just a victim of Villa's treachery. But the soldiers just laughed and fired their rifles in the air and at the ground near Saucedo.

"Dig!" they shouted.

Saucedo dug slowly, as slowly as he could, but his grave deepened nonetheless. Then, inexplicably, or for reasons not remembered by Saucedo's family, the soldiers suddenly rode off, perhaps in search of loot or women, perhaps because they simply were bored with tormenting Saucedo. They carried off Saucedo's goods, and wrecked and burned his store. But he climbed or was pulled out of what had almost become his grave, somehow a survivor. Frightened and robbed of everything, Saucedo soon fled to the United States, where he would make his home in a boxcar in the rail yard in Silvis, Illinois. "That's how grandfather came to America," says his granddaughter, Silvia Saucedo, who now runs a tiny grocery store and tortilla factory on Hero Street, U.S.A.

Angelina and Eduviges Sandoval and their two children suffered greatly during the Mexican Revolution. "I heard stories that they were reduced to eating sawdust," said their son, Tanilo Sandoval. "From what I know, I'm not sure they even had sawdust." It was common practice for the combatant armies to poison wells and irrigation ditches, making water scarce as well. Soldiers—and bandits masquerading as soldiers—stole food and burned crops. The result was *hambruna*: mass starvation. The poor collected rainwater, and ate roaches, weeds, pets, spiders, birds, bugs, and rats — and maybe worse. Prisoners were routinely strung up and left hanging to serve as warnings, and none dared cut them down. Many were shot, many simply maimed but allowed to live — maiming being considered a merciful alternative to execution. Being robbed and humiliated were commonplace occurrences, but also the least of the torments Mexicans might be forced to endure. "In those days, either side could grab you and you couldn't do a damned thing — except leave for the United States," Joseph "Big Joe" Muños said of his parents' reason for fleeing Mexico in 1917.

Women as well as men suffered unspeakable cruelties in the revolution, particularly in the form of rape. "Mother said the women were hidden in holes for days at a time to keep them from the armies," said Joe Terronez, whose parents fled Mexico after the revolution. "The women were kept covered in dirt and filth so no one would find them attractive if they were caught." Josie Soliz remembers that fear reigned when soldiers passed through towns and villages. "Mother told me the women were told to 'pat the tortillas quietly, pat quietly.' If the passing soldiers heard and recognized the sounds, they would rush in and take the food," and likely the women, said Soliz, who was born in León and fled the revolution with her parents. The conflict brutalized Mexicans: "The people grew accustomed to slaughter," wrote muralist and painter Jose Clemente Orozco, "to the most merciless selfishness, to satiating their senses, to pure, unconcealed animality." The revolution's leaders despised the Catholic Church, which had largely supported Huerta, and robbed it of its property and its power to bring order. Many foreign priests, mostly Spanish, were exiled. No church, little government, many angry, hungry armed men.

This near anarchy followed a series of tragedies: Gen. Victoriano Huerta had Francisco Madero assassinated and replaced him as president of Mexico, only to find the nation bankrupt and his regime shunned by most foreign governments. At the same time, Madero's supporters took to arms: Pancho Villa, Emiliano Zapata, Alvaro Obregón, and Venustiano Carranza raised armies and drove

Huerta into exile in July 1914. But then they splintered—Villa teaming with Zapata, Carranza with Obregón. Civil war ensued. So bitter were the rivalries that Carranza suggested at a convention to end the conflict that peace would only come if both he and Villa resigned—Carranza as the "First Chief" and Villa as general of the Army of the North. Villa responded, sarcastically: "I proposed not only that the convention retire Carranza from his post in exchange for me retiring from mine, but that the convention order both of us shot." Carranza quite naturally declined Villa's proposal, and instead sent an army under Obregón to battle Villa. Obregón wrote Carranza: "Let us satisfy their taste for blood until they choke on it" and "a people cannot shed too much blood in defense of their freedoms."

Obregón's and Villa's blood-seeking armies marched to the Bajio, the fertile high plans of Mexico—and the home of Eduviges and Angelina Sandoval. In Celaya, Villa sent waves of cavalry against Obregón's entrenched army. Fighting from positions protected by barbed wire, Obregón's men inflicted terrible losses on Villa's charging horsemen. On both sides casualties were high, prisoner counts low. To save on bullets Villa, far from supply bases, made prisoners stand in files of three, one behind another. That way, one bullet fired through the chest of the first man killed all three. Obregón was no more lenient, but he had plenty of bullets and rope.

In April 1915, Villa dispatched some thirty-five thousand men to León, passing near Angelina's and Eduviges' home near the farming community of Romita. Villa set up a defensive line running twenty kilometers between León and Trinidad. Obregón followed, and his lines formed a rectangle extending roughly from Romita to Santa Ana to Silao to Guanajuato. Both armies confiscated all crops and livestock in the region to sell for ammunition and food. The so-called Battle of León would last forty days and "resemble the long and indecisive battles that European armies were fighting in World War I." After running out of patience with the long wait, Villa attacked Obregón on June 2, 1915, and leveled Silao. Villa forces also attacked Romita, but they were beaten at nearby Santa Ana Hacienda. On June 5, Villa sent his main force against Obregón between La Sandia and Romita. In his memoirs, Villa wrote: "These were strong attacks which my forces made when he [Obregón] was expecting to advance, and his losses and injuries were great." But Villa's cavalry was surrounded near Romita and "had to disperse and abandon their wounded and leave I know not how many prisoners."

A Villa officer recorded this scene, near Angelina and Eduviges' home: "There are a great number of unburied bodies, and their smell has become intolerable. . . . After [the enemy soldiers] our worst enemies are flies, lice and rats. The flies are a beautiful green color, and there are thousands of them, who after eating from the eyes and mouths of the dead attempt to devour our food. The rats are so voracious that in spite of the fact that they have enough to eat with the bodies of the dead, they come and eat our few provisions."

After being routed, Villa's army fled through León, chased by Obregón's soldiers, who took revenge, women, and plunder — including the goods and nearly the life of Dolores Saucedo. The war, the savagery, and the grim aftermath prompted the victorious Gen. Obregón (who lost an arm in the battle and then tried to commit suicide) to write a poem:

I have run after Victory
And I won her
But when I found myself beside her
I felt despair.

The glows of her insignia
Illuminated everything,
The ashes of the dead,
The suffering of the living.

Little was left but despair and gorging green flies, ashes of death, and the suffering of the living. Angelina and Eduviges survived; their daughter, baby Mercedes, did not; and their son, Pedro, died shortly after the war. The prospects for the survivors were grim. "After six years of virtually non-stop warfare," one historian wrote,

Mexico was in chaos. Crops were unharvested, cattle had been exported to buy arms, mines and factories [had] closed. . . . Everywhere there were shortages of food, water, coal and other basics. Agriculture was in crisis as subsistence crops failed and there was no money with which to import grain. Peasants were reduced to eating bran mixed with sawdust or even earth. . . . Famine stalked the land, and in its wake came diseases and pestilence. The countryside was a wasteland of bent and twisted railway tracks, gutted buildings, burned bridges, dynamited factories, carcasses of dead horses or makeshift mass graves for the human fallen. . . . In the cities and towns indigence and destitution were widespread, and hundreds of cripples, limbless men, mutilated veterans and gravely wounded walking hospital cases thronged the streets."

The armies went away, but not the privation. 1916 is remembered as "the year of hunger" in Mexico. No one counted those who died of starvation. A worldwide influenza pandemic claimed hundreds of thousands of lives in Mexico. There is no accurate count of the civilians or combatants who died in the war, although some estimates place the death rate at one in fifteen. One historian estimates that "given the high birthrate during that period, the loss of population because of the war, disease, hunger and emigration was in the millions, with at least 1 million killed." There was no medicine nor doctors, little food or clean water. During the revolution, one out of every two children died in their first year of malaria, whooping cough, yellow fever, or other diseases. Mexico's population declined from 15,160,000 in 1910 to 14,335,000 in 1921. Mexico's new government, led by Carranza, adopted a grand new constitution that promised everyone everything, but in reality it could not pay its own bills, much less feed its starving people or tend to its sick children and limbless men.

Mexicans looked north. Nearly a million Mexicans, maybe more, fled to the United States. The tensions engendered by the revolution, wrote historian Juan R. Garcia, "did not subside when the heavy fighting ended. Weapons were easy to acquire and visible everywhere. The lack of law enforcement and civilian authority led many people to resolve conflicts through violence. . . . The desire for personal safety and security did as much to drive people from their homes as the economic conditions." And America accepted them, although it did so more out of need than compassion. The United States then faced a severe labor shortage. Military service in World War I had taken millions of young American men from their civilian jobs, European immigration had virtually halted, and Congress had enacted legislation barring Japanese and Chinese immigrant workers from entering the country. In recognition of the problem, the U.S. Labor Department exempted Mexican workers from the Immigration Act of 1917. American companies sent recruiters into Mexico, placed ads in Mexican newspapers, and distributed flyers among the populace. Eduviges obtained a permit to look for work, para Estadios Unidos. Angelina and Eduviges bid their families and friends goodbye. Most likely, they paid a final visit to the church where they had been baptized and married and to the grave of their baby daughter Mercedes Then, Eduviges and Angelina and their sickly son, Pedro, joined the exodus.

They headed north to what the Spanish conquistadors called *la Despoblado*," the spoiled lands": a region of harsh deserts guarded by towering mountains. In the myths of the ancients the north was a place of desolation where devils were bound and buried. Author Luis Alberto Urrea, writing in the twenty-first century about Mexicans fleeing to the United States, described the same path Angelina and Eduviges took in 1917:

> They saw many wonders as they traveled north. In some of their ancient beliefs, north was the direction of death. North was the home of winter, and the underworld could be found there. They went from jungle to rain forest to pine forest, from pines to plains to desert and volcanoes. They gawked at the worms of snow on the highest peaks. . . . They crossed little rivers, watched . . . white crosses that had been erected along the highway where their ancestral travelers had perished. The whole way was a ghost road, haunted by

tattered spirits left on the thirsty ground; drivers thrown out of windows, revolutionaries hung from cottonwoods or shot before walls, murdered women tossed in the scrub.

With a permit to look for work in the United States, but little else, Angelina, Eduviges and Pedro started their journey in the winter of 1916–1917. President Carranza ordered railroads — where repaired — to give free passage to refugees heading to the United States. If and when they did travel by train, they likely rode in crowded, windowless boxcars, insufferably hot by day and numbingly cold by night. They probably had little food and water, and toilet facilities were nonexistent. From Romita, they traveled some thirteen kilometers to the rail junction at Silao. From Silao, they probably traveled up the mountains to the state capital, Guanajuato, a once-grand fifteenth century silver mining town. Then, perhaps riding in a boxcar, perhaps walking, they made their way to Dolores Hildalgo, where the Mexican Independence movement began a century earlier. After passing through San Luis Potosi, they entered la Despolado on the so-called Devil's Highway, which took them through Saltillo and Monterrey to Nuevo Laredo on the border with Los Estadios Unidos.

They perhaps had a few pesos loaned them by friends and family. "My father's father was rumored to have had some money and buried it during the revolution," said Tanilo Sandoval. "Maybe he gave them some for their trip, but we don't know for sure." They probably slept in and under boxcars, in fields, in barns and chicken coops, and in shantytowns. What few possessions they had, Eduviges and Angelina carried; and, when trains weren't available, they must have carried Pedro too — until the boy died. "He died on the trail. We don't know when or where," said Jenny Sandoval, a daughter. Angelina and Eduviges buried Pedro along the Devil's Highway, in that same place of desolation where the ancient devils lay buried, covering the grave with rocks so the coyotes couldn't dig up the body, and then erecting a cross fashioned from branches over it. Surely they prayed and wept as they performed this grim task; perhaps they thought about returning home. But there was no hope, no nothing, to the south. So they kept going north.

CHAPTER FOUR

Red Boxcar

We only came to sleep,
We only came to dream:
It is not true; it is not true that we came to live on the earth.
— Mexica poem

Starving, grieving, clad in rags, Angelina and Eduviges Sandoval reached the desert border town of Laredo-Nuevo Laredo in April 1917. Refugees overwhelmed the already impoverished town, and the bankrupt Mexican government was powerless to help. While the weather remained mild back in their home some five hundred miles to the south, the April temperatures in the deserts around Laredo climbed into the nineties in the daytime and dipped into the forties at night, and a shanty town of tin-and-paper shacks offered little shelter to refugees. But Laredo offered hope — American companies were hiring able-bodied Mexican men, and Eduviges obtained an official green card that allowed him to work in the United States. An agent for the Chicago, Rock Island, and Pacific Railroad spotted Eduviges. He was thirty years old, mustachioed, strong, tall, polite, and well tanned beneath a worn cowboy hat. American companies preferred married men because they thought them more stable. The agent offered Eduviges a job, and paid ten cents each so Angelina and Eduviges could take the required showers and be dusted with lice powder before crossing the Rio Grande River into the United States. And the railroad agent gave them train tickets to Silvis, Illinois.

Their journey to Silvis was long (nearly fourteen hundred miles), slow, and arduous. One can only imagine their apprehensions and anxieties, their sense of vulnerability and isolation: strangers in a strange land, they spoke no English and, apart from the inhabitants of impoverished Mexican settlements along the rail line, they encountered few who spoke Spanish. The train passed through five states — Texas, Oklahoma, Kansas, Missouri, Iowa — before reaching Illinois. At Davenport, Iowa, they crossed the Mississippi River into Rock Island, Illinois, over a steel, double-deck bridge. From there, they had just a short trip east and north along the Mississippi River into the little railroad town of Silvis. Eduviges first went to work at the Chicago and Rock Island rail yard in Silvis in September 1917.

Angelina and Eduviges found refuge in the nine hundred-acre Silvis steam locomotive rail yard where a "Little Mexico" had been created. Railroad officials gave them, for their new home, a boxcar without wheels. Railroad workers painted the boxcars red because they believed the bright color cheered the refugees. Red boxcar aside, the scenery was bleak. South of the rail yard was Silvis' main street, 1st Avenue, featuring a collection of small shops — Dunbeck's drug store and post office, the Silvis Buffet and Bar, a bakery, barber shop, and several taverns and pool halls. South of 1st Avenue rose a hillside where working class Italians, Poles, Irish, Croatians, and other European immigrants lived in little frame houses. This neighborhood was off-limits to Mexicans and blacks; real estate brokers, landlords, and community residents opposed selling or renting property to Mexicans because of fears about their character and cleanliness. But Mexican children were allowed to attend McKinley Elementary School, also located on the hill, which offered English language classes to its foreign students. About one mile north on a bluff overlooking the Mississippi River stood the Watertown State Hospital (formerly the Illinois Western Hospital for the Insane), a fenced four-story brownstone facility for the mentally ill. About one mile to the west, barges and riverboats trafficked the slow-moving Mississippi River. To the east lay the prairie, overgrown with thickets of oak and rosebud bushes and traversed by railroad tracks leading to mighty Chicago.

In the sky, ducks, herons, wrens, bald eagles, hawks, black crows, red robins, crimson cardinals, and gangly white pelicans flew. Huge flocks of starlings sometimes filled the air. Fox, raccoons, skunks, rabbits, and deer raided the Mexicans' precious gardens. Angelina and Eduviges woke some days to morning fogs, some days to torrential rains or heavy snowfalls. Some days rain fell but landed as ice. Winds howled across the prairie in every season, and violent thunderstorms and tornados periodically thrashed the region. Temperatures plummeted below zero in the winter and soared above one hundred degrees in the summer, and the humidity was always high, especially in comparison to the dry and relatively mild climate of the high desert where Angelina and Eduviges had previously lived.

And there was always noise, smoke, and dust. Steam-driven locomotives pulled long trains that rumbled in and out of the rail yard, day and night, seven days a week. Engines snorted, belched, wheezed, and whistled on the main lines, on the switch spurs, in the giant repair shop, and in the huge roundhouse. Black smoke bellowed from multiple coal-fired engines, and coal cars seemed to be everywhere. Thousands of workers, speaking many languages, came and went around the clock. Most workers used the 9th Street viaduct to cross over countless tracks to go between their jobs and their homes. But the Mexicans didn't leave the yard to go home. They lived there.

In the midst of this tumultuous setting, overalls and cotton dresses flapped on clothes lines tied between boxcars, fighting a losing battle with the swirling soot and coal dust. Little boys darted everywhere, throwing knives, shooting slingshots, rolling marbles, and swinging rough baseball bats at homemade baseballs. Women gossiped in Spanish while they stooped to pull weeds from their vegetable gardens, or scrubbed stacks of homespun clothes on washboards. Missing at first glance were young girls — always shielded from view, hidden inside their boxcar homes from the dangers that history had always brought their way.

Hostility surrounded the red boxcars in Little Mexico. World War I triggered patriotism that spawned nationalism that led to nativism. The German government stirred anti-Mexican sentiments when, in 1917, it sent the Zimmerman Telegram proposing that Mexico enter the war against the United States. In exchange, the Germans promised the return to Mexico of California, Texas, and the other territories lost in the Mexican-American War. Mexicans were also suspect because many Americans viewed Russia's Bolshevik Revolution of November 1917 as a cousin to the Mexican Revolution.

Mexican immigrants like Eduviges and Angelina also met with hostility — and, sometimes, violence — from racist groups like the Klu Klux Klan. Reborn in 1915, the Klan reached the height of its of power over the next ten years, with as many as four million members bent on "uniting native-born white Christians for concerted action in the preservation of American institutions and the supremacy of the white race." Against the depredations of the Klan and likeminded organizations, Mexicans in America were largely defenseless: they were officially aliens, and the bankrupt Mexican government was virtually powerless to protect its citizens within Mexico, much less the refugees who'd fled to the United States.

American leaders were hardly sympathetic. President Woodrow Wilson — who allowed D. W. Griffith's tribute to the Klan, *The Birth of a Nation*, to be shown in the White House — was "in essence a white supremacist." A Wilson biographer recorded that "a bloody tide of lynchings and race riots in 1917, 1918 and 1919 seemed to confirm that the administration's attitude had licensed hatred and bigotry." The Harding Administration was little better. The *New York Times*, in a 1922 editorial, wrote "the killing of Mexicans without provocation is so common as to pass almost unnoticed." The Mexican government's efforts to demand protection for its citizens usually fell on deaf ears. The *Heraldo* of Mexico City complained: "It is thoroughly irritating that while in our country American citizens enjoy ample guarantees and when anything happens to them it is settled by the United States consuls, in that country . . . Mexicans are . . . being killed without any effort by the American authorities to punish the murders." Calvin Coolidge succeeded to the American presidency when Harding died in 1925, and although he "abhorred" the KKK, he couldn't bring himself to condemn the Klan "or take any actions to create more harmonious race relations."

Still, starving Mexicans fled north as chaos in the world generated opportunity. In addition to the wheel-less red boxcar, the railroad gave Eduviges a job at 35 cents an hour, low wages by American standards but a fortune to Mexicans who'd survived poverty, war, and starvation in their homeland. They finally had an income and a roof over their heads, humble as it was.

Angelina must have found this new world especially intimidating. The men who ran the railroad knew a little Spanish and talked to Eduviges, and he could read maps and newspapers written in Spanish. Angelina couldn't read or write in any language. She wouldn't and couldn't talk to strangers. She never left the boxcar community except on Sundays when everyone walked a couple of miles to St. Mary's Catholic Church in neighboring East Moline. Even there, the other parishioners weren't uniformly welcoming. Eventually those weekly Sunday morning trips out of "Little Mexico" ended after the Mexicans built their own church out of two boxcars in the yard.

The Mexicans lived in three different yards at Silvis. Eduviges and Angelina were one of fifteen families who lived in boxcars in the east — or third — yard. The railroad gave the families access to the yard's lumber supply, from which furniture was made. The men cut doors and windows in the boxcars, and installed wood-burning stoves. Four or five families shared one water well and pump — but the boxcars were without running water, electricity, or plumbing. In the Roman Catholic tradition, most families had many children. Eduviges and Angelina had ten children born in the United States — six boys and four girls. Each family had a garden that was tended diligently by the wives and children. The families' children sawed railroad ties into blocks sixteen to twenty inches long that were split and burned for cooking and for heat in the bitterly cold prairie winters.

Eduviges (*center*) and Angelina Sandoval (*left*) and family. Photo courtesy of Georgia and Tanilo Sandoval.

The men worked in the Rock Island Line's shops, blacksmith yard, or on section gangs that traveled far and wide. The women cared for the children, sewed, washed huge amounts of laundry, ground corn into tamales and tortillas, and canned tomatoes and hung peppers out to dry for use in the winter. The women and children hauled water from the pumps to cook and to wash clothes. Makeshift tents strung up around the wells offered family members privacy so they could bathe. The water was always cold, especially during the winter months. On winter mornings, ice covered the water buckets, and the Mexicans used picks to break the ice. Women seemed to bear a child nearly every year in their boxcars. Midwives and neighbor women helped with the births. A doctor came the day after to sign a birth certificate. Little medicine was available.

Using the railroad's lumber, the Mexicans built a band shell, and formed a band that was regionally known for its Mexican music. They also built a baseball diamond on the northern edge of the rail yard. "Baseball was a new sport to the Mexicans," said Joe Terronez, perhaps the last child born in the rail yard. "But they took to it real fast, and they loved it and played well." He said watching baseball games between the yard teams and other teams were "major social events for everyone" in the yard — except the girls. Girls never attended the baseball games or the concerts in the band shell. They weren't allowed to shoot marbles, visit neighbors, and listen to radios. "The girls couldn't go any place, or do anything, except [go] to school and church and . . . work in the garden," said Teresa Sierra, who lived in the rail yard from age six months until she was twelve in 1929. "Our parents wouldn't let us play with nobody. We had to pin our dresses at the neck and our dresses had to cover our ankles. If we weren't home from school within twenty-five minutes after classes were over we'd be in big trouble. Mom said Dad would kill us if we didn't obey, and we never knew there was any other way."

Mexico is considered one of the most Catholic countries in the world, and the Mexicans in the yard brought their religion with them into the yard. All the families dressed for and walked to mass every Sunday morning. "Every Sunday, no matter the weather, Mom would get us dressed and Dad would lead us on foot to St.

The Corporation Musical Mexicana Hildalgo band, led by conductor Manual Macias, is pictured here in front of two boxcars pulled together in the Rock Island railroad yard in Silvis, 1925. Two years later, the Mexican community used the joined boxcars to create Our Lady of Guadalupe Church, Silvis's first church. Photo courtesy of Peter Macias.

Mary's Church," about a mile and a half away in neighboring East Moline, said Teresa Sierra. "It was fine in the summer, but in the winter it was terrible. We almost froze, it was so far." Discrimination followed them, even to mass. White church members sometimes evicted Mexicans from pews, and sometimes Mexicans listened to mass standing outside in the cold. The Mexicans decided in the late 1920s that they needed their own church. So the men got together and dragged two boxcars together. They knocked out the adjoining middle walls. The entire Mexican community, including their band, turned out for the dedication of the Church of Our Lady of Guadalupe, the virgin patron saint of Mexico, on Easter Sunday, 1928. "It was the first church in Silvis, and it was Mexicans who built it," said Joe Terronez. The church stood about fifty yards west of the Sandovals' boxcar.

Just to the east of their boxcar was the rail yard dump. Everyone — the railroad and the residents of Little Mexico — used it. "They dumped everything and all kinds of things from the yard in that dump," said Joe Terronez. "They put things in that dump that they probably couldn't just throw away today. Nobody even thought about it." Despite the dump, the lack of electricity and running water, the frigid winters and the hot, humid summers, the red boxcar served as something of an oasis — until Angelina and Eduviges and their children once again found themselves in another "No Man's Land" between warring factions.

CHAPTER FIVE

No Man's Land, Again

Save us from the time of trial
And deliver us from evil.
— From the Lord's Prayer

On the morning of Saturday, July 1, 1922, Eduviges and Angelina Sandoval locked themselves and their two sons, Joseph, three, and Frank, two, inside their boxcar. A small army of guards carrying rifles, pistols, and shotguns had arrived just as the sun rose at 5:30 A.M. The Brotherhood of Railroad Carmen of the Railway Employees' Department of the American Federation of Labor had voted by a 57 percent margin to strike. When the night shift ended at 10:00 A.M., the night crew walked out, and the day shift did not report. Singing labor songs, the night shift paraded across the pedestrian viaduct over the rail lines into downtown Silvis where other union members joined them for a solidarity march through town. Eduviges, although a union member, did not sing the songs or join the parade. Nor did he strike.

For nearly five years, the red boxcar in the Rock Island's Silvis rail yard had provided a safe haven for Eduviges and Angelina. Eduviges' work was hard, but steady. Regular income allowed them to send a little money back to relatives in Mexico, and save a few dollars in a Moline bank. They had their own garden on the edge of the yard and grew corn and squash and other vegetables. They made friends among the other Mexicans, and attended church regularly. Two years after their arrival in America, they resumed having children. But no matter their wishes, peace was not their destiny.

The strike's timing couldn't have been worse. Angelina was almost full-term pregnant. The couple's first American-born daughter, Jenny, would be born eleven days after the strike began. If he struck, Eduviges would lose his income and, perhaps more importantly, the family home — the boxcar the railroad provided him. Deportation was possible. Just the year before, between two hundred thousand and four hundred thousand Mexican nationals had been forced to return to Mexico — a grim prospect considering the dismal Mexican economy. Any idea that his own government of Mexico could help him should he strike was unimaginable. Eduviges chose living as a strikebreaker in a boxcar in an armed camp rather than a voluntary or forcible return to Mexico.

Of the Chicago, Rock Island and Pacific's 11,480 employees nationwide represented by the striking union, 8,150 — 71 percent — walked off the job. The walkout became the largest strike to date in U.S. history. Most of Eduviges' fellow workers — blacksmiths, boilermakers, electrical workers, and sheet-metal workers — walked off the job to protest pay cuts that took effect that day. An estimated fourteen hundred Rock Island Railroad employees struck the Silvis yard. The union claimed that more than four hundred thousand workers struck nationwide against multiple railroads that day.

The background of the strike was complex. President Wilson had nationalized the railroads during World War I, and workers' pay and benefits grew while the federal government was in charge. More importantly, the Wilson administration encouraged unionization of railroad workers. When the government returned the railroads to private ownership in March 1920, the owners wanted to cut pay, benefits, and — most significantly — the newly won power of the unions. The railroad barons found an ally in Republican Senator

Warren G. Harding of Ohio, who was elected President in November 1920 on a campaign pledge to return the nation to "normalcy." To the railroad barons, normalcy meant no union power that could challenge owners' rights.

Eduviges knew the risks of strikebreaking were high, perhaps fatal. Just eight days before the rail workers struck, a local newspaper ran this set of front-page headlines: "ILLINOIS MINERS IN A BLOODY WAR" / "TWENTY-SIX KNOWN TO HAVE BEEN KILLED IN CONFLICTS AT HERRIN." The June 22, 1922, Davenport Democrat added: "List of Dead Is Being Constantly Increased; Bodies were scattered Over an Area 15 Miles Square; Three Were Found Hanging by Ropes from Trees and Others Beaten; Men Attempting to Escape Were Massacred." The massacre was a warning to strikebreakers. The dead were coal miners who'd defied a strike called by the United Mine Workers. After a truce was arranged, fifty men came out of the mine and were marched to Herrin while a mob that included women and children taunted and spit on the strikebreakers and armed men hit them with pistols and rifle butts.

At this juncture, the president of the local union drove up, jumped out of a car, and said: "Listen, don't you go killing those fellows on a public highway. There are too many women and children around to do that. Take them over in the woods and give it to them. Kill all you can." The mob marched the strikebreakers into the woods and told them to run for their lives. As they ran rifle and pistol shots rang out. Some were killed on the spot; others were caught and shot or hanged. Six strikebreakers were captured and taken to the Herrin Cemetery and yoked together, then shot. If they moved, they were shot again. If they still moved, their throats were slit. One of the mob urinated on several bodies. The striking coal miners sought an alliance with the striking rail workers. United Mine Workers national President John L. Lewis called the wage cut imposed on the railroad workers "outrageous, unwarrantable and unjustifiable." Lewis called for the miners and rail shopmen to protect "their mutual interests" and "exert their collective strength."

To protect non-striking workers, the Rock Island Railroad hired almost seven hundred private guards, who were often "tough thugs." The railroads brought strikebreakers in by train, and housed them in boxcars and tent cities. Food and tobacco and other goods were furnished inside the heavily guarded yards. By the end of July, more than twenty-two hundred deputy United States marshals had been appointed and National Guard troops were on duty in seven states. By August 21, the federal government had increased the number of deputy federal marshals working the strike to 3,195, including 251 in Illinois. The railroad hired one guard for every ten employees who continued working.

Most white union members struck. They ran the union, and benefited more from union membership than did Mexicans and other minorities. Eduviges and other Mexican workers were regularly rejected by shopcraft unions and prevented from moving up to skilled positions. Because he did not strike, the railroad called Eduviges a "loyal employee" and paid him a bonus. President Harding told Congress that all men had a right to work, and none had a right to bar Eduviges and others from working. Men such as Eduviges, who refused to strike "have been cruelly attacked and wounded or killed," Harding told Congress. But union-leaning newspapers denounced them in the harshest terms, of which "strikebreakers" was the mildest. Eduviges dared not leave the rail yard while the strike lasted — and the strike lasted seven months. It was not safe for strikebreakers to walk the streets. Union supporters jeered, spat on, tarred and feathered — and even murdered — strikebreakers.

Both sides resorted to violence. One week after the strike began, in Clinton, Iowa — just thirty miles north of Silvis — railroad guards were escorting workers into the Illinois Central Railroad yard when union members tried to stop the "scabs." "The guards began cursing us and as they did so they drew their guns and began to fire directly at us," striker William F. Horn told the Davenport Democrat. Horn reported some fifty shots being fired. Striking rail worker James Fitzgerald was shot in the leg. His twelve-year-old son, James Fitzgerald Jr., was shot in the chest and killed. A passerby was shot in both legs. That same day, in Bloomington, Illinois, according to a New York Times report, "a mob of between 200 and 300 men raided the shop plant and drove off every employee they could find by threatening the men's lives." Strikers conducted similar raids on rail shops in Iowa, Michigan, and Wisconsin. A passenger train running at 40 miles an hour near Hutchinson, Kansas, ran off the tracks. Nine passengers were hurt, and sabotage was suspected.

Federal judges in Council Bluffs, Iowa, and Chicago issued injunctions ordering the striking unions to not interfere with train operations. One federal judge declared that the federal courts represented "the last bulwark between the people and Communism, Bolshevism and anarchy." The entire Illinois National Guard was activated July 8 and ordered to be ready for deployment wherever strike violence might occur. "We are now prepared to nip in the bud any trouble that may show its head," Col. Frank Taylor of the Adjutant General's Office said in the July 9, 1922, Davenport Democrat. "The state is almost an armed camp from end to end."

Perhaps most frightening to Angelina and Eduviges, in mid-July guards and strikers on the picket line outside the Silvis yard exchanged between twenty-five and thirty gunshots. One person, a policeman, was slightly injured, but the railroad and town residents demanded that Governor Len Small declare marshal law and send in the National Guard. National Guard units had already been called out elsewhere in the state. But instead of National Guard soldiers, more deputy U.S. marshals and sheriff's deputies from Rock Island County were dispatched to Silvis yard. As the summer wore on, some strikers tried to sabotage railroad equipment and lines. Strikers were accused of ripping up rail spikes and causing a passenger car derailment near Gary, Indiana. National Guard troops were ordered into Joliet, Illinois — about one hundred miles east of Silvis — after the August 5, 1922, shooting deaths of striker Frank Levino and a railroad guard. On August 9, National Guardsmen fired on the picket line in Joliet.

In the midst of the strike, President Harding addressed Congress on August 18, 1922, declaring that "lawlessness and violence in a hundred places have revealed the failure of the striking unions to hold their forces to law observance." The president added, "Even officers of the federal government have been assaulted, humiliated, and hindered in their duties." Members of Congress rose and applauded when he told them "I am resolved to use all the power of the government to maintain transportation and sustain the right of men to work." He accused strikers of "mobocracy" and said they were starting to disrupt interstate commerce.

The president tried to mediate between the unions and the railroad owners. The unions agreed to one of his proposals, but the railroads rejected the settlement because it would have restored seniority to returning workers. The railroads wanted all returning men to be rehired as new employees, losing valuable seniority rights.

In late August, Attorney General Harry M. Daugherty got U.S. District Court Judge James H. Wilkerson, a recent Harding appointee, to issue a sweeping injunction against the striking unions claiming the strike interrupted the delivery of U.S. mail and interstate commerce. The injunction effectively broke the back of the strike, although wildcat strikes against railroads lasted several more years. The union officially settled with the Rock Island Railroad in February 1923, but by that time most of the striking union members either had been "rehired" by the railroad, had gone to work for other railroads, or had found employment elsewhere. "The walkout had serious effects on the operation of the railroad and proved disastrous not only to the company but also to the employees for the length of time it lasted," wrote William Edward Hayes in his history of the Rock Island Railroad. "It was, from the outset, a lost cause for the strikers. New men were hired to man the shops and strikers were shut out. By September 1922 most of them were willing to call it quits and come back to work. But those for whom jobs could be found had to fall in behind the new workers insofar as seniority was concerned."

By the end of the strike, Eduviges was a much more senior employee of the railroad. His seniority date remained September 1917, while returning strikers were given starting dates of September 1922 or later. "When the Depression came and the railroad went into bankruptcy, dad never got laid off," said his son, Tanilo Sandoval. "His seniority dated to 1917. He always worked [during the Great Depression] and we always had food on the table." Job promotions were based largely on seniority, but Eduviges never applied for any promotions. "He never used his seniority to try to get anyone else's job." Tanilo said his father worked the worst shifts, the coldest nights, the dirtiest jobs, and never complained or asked for a job inside the roundhouse or the locomotive repair shop. When the Great Depression came, and Eduviges kept his job while most lost theirs, neighbors — and even hobos — could always get a meal at the Sandovals' house. "Mom understood hunger, and dad understood how lucky he was to have work," Tanilo said.

CHAPTER SIX

Odd Child Out

"Thirty-seven — not counting Mexicans. "
— Gunfighter King Fisher's response when asked how
many men he had killed.

E very school morning, the many children of 2nd Street poured
out of their families' little houses. Most of the boys climbed
straight up the steep hill on the east side of 2nd Street, cut through
neighbors' yards, then clambered up steep cement stairs to McKinley School on the east side of 6th Street. The school, which offered
classes up to 8th grade, overlooked the bustling rail yard and the
Mississippi River in the distance. The girls walked unpaved 2nd
Street to 1st Avenue (Silvis' main street), then east to 6th Street,
and climbed back up the steep hill two blocks to the school. The
children passed hundreds of railroad workers — including their fathers, uncles, brothers, and godfathers — heading toward a large
pedestrian viaduct at 9th Street and 1st Avenue. The viaduct offered the only safe passage over the many tracks that fed into the
rail yard's roundhouse. Against the grain, one child walked alone
and in agony.

Tony Pompa lived with his family in a small, one-story house at

184 2nd Street. Deeply religious, his parents wanted special school-ing for Tony. They couldn't afford tuition, but talked the priests at St. Mary's school into accepting him — and later his brother, Frank — as charity cases. Tony hated it all — school in general, being a charity case, the nuns' discipline, speaking nothing but English, and not being with his friends. Most especially, he hated being the only Mexican kid in class. He pleaded every day with his parents to let him leave St. Mary's and go to McKinley, but they said no. His parents wanted him to have a special, religious-based education. Tony didn't want to be special or different. "My brother just wanted to be one of the boys — and spend a lot of time with the girls," said Frank Pompa.

Even before his birth, world events determined Tony's fate. The depression of 1921 — one of the six worst in American history — cost some six million Americans their jobs. Chants went up: "American jobs for Americans" — especially jobs for returning World War I veterans. Mexicans were the first to be fired. Mexican railroad em-ployees faced a double whammy. The U.S. government had na-tionalized the nation's railroads during the war, but private owner-ship of the Rock Island Line was restored on February 29, 1920. Management believed the government had padded the railroad's employment, and — in the first year after privatization — cut the number of employees at the Rock Island from 45,950 to 34,531. Juan Pompa was among those who lost his job.

For Mexicans in the U.S., the effects of the 1921 depression were "devastating." Some 100,000 of the 478,383 Mexicans immi-grants counted in the 1920 census lost their jobs. Unemployment, increased discrimination, and forced and voluntary repatriation caused some two hundred thousand Mexicans to leave the United States, reducing many Mexicans to a "state of semi-pauperism." Unemployed Mexicans were encouraged to return to their home-land. Sometimes they were forcibly repatriated to Mexico in hopes of reducing unemployment and the burden placed by the jobless on charitable programs and institutions in the United States. The

federal government reinstituted its waiver of immigration restrictions for Mexicans, saying it didn't want to set a precedent of helping indigent foreigners. So, Juan Pompa and his wife and daughters returned to Leon, Guanajuato, in central Mexico. His son, Frank, doesn't know if his father returned voluntarily or was forcibly repatriated.

But it's doubtful the Pompas went back to Mexico willingly, given how difficult it had been for them to reach the United States in the first place, according to the family history remembered by Frank Pompa: Juan Pompa was sixteen when he fled to the United States in the midst of the Mexican Revolution. Juan's brother-in-law, Julian Segura, had already "crossed" into the United States, and had sent word to Juan that there was work for Mexican men on the railroad in Kansas. Juan promised his young wife, Maria, that he would return to Leon as soon as the revolution ended. Maria told him: "Where you leave me is where you will find me when you come back."

That was a pledge she wouldn't be able to keep. Shortly after Juan left for the United States, Maria learned she was pregnant and followed her husband north to Juarez, just across the Rio Grande River from El Paso, Texas. She had no money, friends, or place to live, and no means to cross into America. She lived on the streets of Juarez's shantytown as a pregnant teenage beggar. Maria somehow got word to Juan and her brother, Julian, who drove a Model T Ford from Kansas to far West Texas to rescue his sister. But it was too late for the baby, a girl named Semona, who died in childbirth on the streets of Juarez. Maria buried the baby girl in an unmarked pauper's grave somewhere in the border town. "We don't know where my sister is buried," Frank Pompa said.

Julian brought Maria to Kansas where she was reunited with Juan. In 1918, in Fort Dodge, their daughter, Clara, was born. The family moved to Silvis, where the Chicago, Rock Island and Pacific Railroad hired Juan as a maintenance worker. The railroad gave the young family a boxcar in which to live in the sprawling rail yard. Times were relatively good during economic boom immediately following the war. The Rock Island Railroad reached its all-time high gross revenues of $142 million in 1920. There was work for everyone — until the depression of 1921.

When the Pompas and other Mexicans returned to Mexico, they found little opportunity in their native land, where wages were one-fifth what they were in the United States. The country's farms produced less food than in pre-revolutionary 1910. Hunger, disease, unemployment, corruption, and poverty thrived. When men could find jobs they were paid as little as twelve centavos (six cents, U.S.) a day for men, while women got six centavos. In the midst of this poverty, the Pompas' first-born son, Tony, was born in Leon on January 17, 1924 — a citizen of Mexico. When the 1921 depression ended — and when the Rock Island Railroad (and steel mills, sugar beet farms, and auto plants) needed cheap labor again — Mexicans flooded north across the border. Juan and his family returned to the United States and the rail yard in Silvis in 1925 when Tony was one year old.

The 1920s "roared" for many Americans. Women got the right to vote. Alcohol was outlawed, but was readily available. Sports figures such as Babe Ruth, Jack Dempsey, and Red Grange became national icons — thanks in part to the establishment of new commercial radio stations. But times were tough for Mexican immigrants in the United States. Anti-immigrant sentiment was rife and led to the 1924 Immigration Act, inspired, in part, by Madison Grant's book *The Passing of the Great Race*. Historian Carey McWilliams wrote: "Mexicans were a 'conquered' people . . . whose culture had been under incessant attack for many years and whose character and achievements, as a people, have been consistently disparaged. . . . Mexicans . . . show evidence of the spiritual defeatism which so often arises when a cultural minority is annexed to an alien culture." Baby Tony Pompa, a natural-born Mexican citizen, was an "alien" in America. He would fight to the death in order to prove otherwise.

Powers unknown changed Tony's life again when he was just five. In 1929, just before the Great Depression began, Silvis officials demanded that the boxcar settlement be shut down — the Mexicans, they said, should pay property taxes like everyone else. The Pompas and other Mexicans moved to unpaved 2nd Street on the extreme west end of town into an area that had once served as a dump. Juan Pompas used his life savings to buy a tiny, one-story house at 184 2nd Street that had no running water, plumbing, or electricity. The poorly insulated one-story, wood-frame house was heated by a stove that burned sawed-off railroad ties. Juan and Maria arranged to have Tony attend St. Mary's Catholic School in nearby East Moline. "We were charity cases and everybody let us know it in different ways," said Tony's younger brother, Frank, who was born in 1930. "Tony hated school, and hated not being with the other Mexican kids. He cut more days than he attended. I remember having to go to the principal's office and being asked: 'Where is your brother?' How should I know? He was almost seven years older and he didn't tell me what he did or where he went." Historian Thomas P. Carter wrote that the Mexican tradition of machismo resulted in many Mexican American boys "skipping school, liking girls, disliking school, being impudent, and getting bad grades." That was Tony. He was a star baseball player on the local Mexican team, and a star with the girls. He was probably the best looking of the boys in "Little Mexico." He liked baseball and girls, and hated school and the nuns who ran it. He hated being a charity case, and being different.

In the spring of 1941, Tony quit school and got a job as a janitor at the nearby Rock Island Arsenal. Tony thought it was a great job, and his friends envied him — until arsenal officials discovered he was Mexican born and thus not an American citizen. They fired him. Despairing and believing that joining the U.S. military would entitle him to American citizenship, he tried to enlist in the army. But his parents refused and tried unsuccessfully to get him to return to school. At sixteen, he couldn't join the army without parental permission. So, in the summer of 1941, Tony persuaded a neighbor, a Mrs. Lopez, to help. She told an army recruiter that she was Tony's mother and signed papers allowing "Tony Lopez" to join the army. All during boot camp, all during World War II, all the rest of his life — and during two burials — he was known as Tony Lopez.

Tony Pompa

Tony fared well in the army. On December 3, 1941, he passed a test to be a gunner on a B-24 Liberator bomber in the U.S. Army Air Forces. "Being an aerial gunner is my dream. The only problem is that I have to sign up for four more years (in the Army). Oooie," he wrote his sister, Clara. Tony signed papers extending his enlistment by three years just four days before the Japanese attack on the military installations at Pearl Harbor. Tony trained at an airfield in South Dakota, where he met and married an Anglo woman, Dolores. They soon had a son, Tony Jr., and when Tony was shipped overseas, Dolores was pregnant again with their daughter, Sharon. Tony transferred to the 717th Squadron — the "Flying Horsemen" — of the 449th Bomb Group stationed at Fort Bruning, Nebraska. In early December 1943, he and the other air crews flew their B-24 bombers from Nebraska to Kansas to Florida to Brazil to various airfields in Africa. From one stop, near Casablanca, he wrote home that the "transportation here reminds me of Mexico — horses and carts." He said the poverty was even worse than on 2nd Street in Silvis.

The 449th's final destination was the former German-held airfield at Grottaglie, in far southern Italy. First Lieutenant Damon Turner, the unit's official historian, kept a diary. On December 28, he wrote: "Conditions . . . are bad. There are no lights, no latrines, poor food, no beds, bombed-out buildings, no heat, no nothing." The next day, Turner wrote: "At Grottaglie it's become a matter of survival. What we would give for a bath." On January 4, he wrote: "Everyone lives in two large stone buildings. Gasoline stoves made of empty cans give heat but are dangerous." Tony's unit saw its first combat on January 8. "A solemn occasion," Turner wrote; "Today the 449th went into action. . . . How happy we were to see all our planes return." January 9: "They must need us badly. The target was Zara, Yugoslavia. Seventeen of our planes made the attack, which was unsuccessful due to overcast." Turner complained of no mail, long lines at the latrines, no showers, shaving out of helmets filled with cold water, and bad food. More bad news on January 14: "The group lost its first aircraft in combat. . . . A ship . . . was hit by falling bombs from another aircraft." The next day, Turner wrote: "Everyone is dirty, tired, sleepy and hungry."

On January 17, 1944, Tony turned twenty. It was cold and wet, and there was no birthday cake. He wrote home that he'd "almost forgotten" his birthday. He was busy. That day his unit dropped sixty-five tons of five hundred-pound bombs on Pisa to help prepare for a major Allied offensive. On January 22, the Allies safely landed more than thirty-six thousand men along with their vehicles and equipment on the beach near Anzio, meeting almost no resistance. The Allied army was less than forty miles from Nazi-occupied Rome. Tony was promoted to gunnery sergeant on the B-24 bomber known as "Sinner's Dream." He wrote home: "Our plane has an almost life-like drawing of a nearly naked woman in black silk panties. I've gotten into the habit of patting her just for luck."

On January 31, Tony's unit bombed German positions near Aviano. The Germans resisted with hundreds of fighters and fierce antiaircraft artillery. The official record of the 717th said the 449th experienced "intense, accurate, heavy flak. . . . One B-24 was seen to go down apparently out of control over the target after a flak hit. Nine parachutes were seen to open from this ship. The plane was seen to go into a steep dive, level momentarily, then crash into a mountainside." The lost B-24 was Sinner's Dream.

The bomber carried ten men, but just nine parachutes opened. A crew member later told the family that Tony's parachute opened inside the plane and snagged on equipment, and that Tony got out of the way to let his crew mates jump. One of the surviving crewmen watched the plane burn for hours. "There definitely wasn't anything left of my brother — just his dog tags," said his sister, Clara. The dog tags identified him as Tony Lopez.

The army buried Tony in Italy under the name Tony Lopez. When they disinterred his body in 1948 for shipment home, the army contacted his widow, Dolores. She had remarried and didn't want Tony's body shipped to her, so she told the army to ship the body to Silvis. A casket labeled "Tony Lopez" arrived in January 1949, and the army buried him at the U.S. Military Cemetery on Arsenal Island under a tombstone that said "Sgt. Tony Lopez." "After the war it took forever to straighten out his records . . . to get the Army to change his name," said his brother, Frank. "To them, he was Tony Lopez. They knew no different." Today, the war memorial on the corner of Hero Street and 1st Avenue in Silvis lists him as Tony Pompa. The army finally agreed to change his grave marker at Arsenal Island — where Tony had lost his job because he wasn't an American — to Tony Pompa. Frank said: "My brother died for America so he could be an American."

CHAPTER SEVEN

New Suit for Graduation

In peace, sons bury their fathers. In war, fathers
bury their sons.
— Herodotus

On a steaming summer night in 1935, eight-year-old Joe Terronez was alone and in big trouble. The boys on 2nd Street
had spotted him after sunset, on their turf. The boys of Little Mexico — 2nd Street, 3rd Street, and 4th Street — were rivals. Joe lived
over the hill on 4th Street — so, after dark, he was fair game. The
boys liked to box, and the 2nd Street boys spent hours working out
on a makeshift punching bag. But they much preferred human
targets, and this night it looked like Joe would be the punching bag.
He tried to run, but older and faster boys grabbed Joe, pinned his
arms, and began punching. Then, from somewhere, came 14 —
year — old Frank Sandoval. "Stop!" he told the other boys. "He's
okay — he's my compadre." "Sorry Frankie," the other boys said.
"We didn't know you were Frank's compadre," they added, and
freed him. "That was a high honor to be an older boy's compadre,"
Joe said. "I knew him a little from church and school, but he was a

lot older and I didn't know until that night that I was his compadre," Joe said. "He said, 'I like you and anytime you want to come
over here you just mention my name.' So I could go almost any
place because Frank Sandoval was my compadre. That meant a lot
to me, and it still does [seventy years later]." Terronez honors all
the granite reliefs of faces that peer out of the war memorial on
Hero Street, U.S.A., but it is his compadre Frank Sandoval whose
memory he most cherishes.

Frank's older brother, Joseph, was adept at language and numbers,
and quickly learned English and arithmetic. Their parents, Eduviges and Angelina Sandoval, couldn't read or write English, so as
soon as Joe learned English, Eduviges assigned him to help read
their mail, fill out government forms, and deal with any paperwork
needed by Eduviges' employer. "Dad designated Joe as the bright
one in the family," said Tanilo Sandoval, one of Frank and Joe's
younger brothers. "Since Joe was the bright one, dad made Frank
the workhorse. And dad knew how to make people work."

To Frank, two years Joe's junior, fell the duty of working odd
jobs to help bring in extra nickels and dimes to help feed the family
of twelve during the Great Depression. Frank, with help from the
family's younger children, tended and tilled the family garden,
where they grew corn, squash, tomatoes, pumpkin, eggplant, and
other crops. Even before he was ten, Frank worked fourteen-hour
days picking onions for five cents a bushel in the sweltering, humid
Iowa fields just across the Mississippi River. When he was thirteen,
Frank worked as a janitor at McKinley School. When other students
went home to play, Frank swept the halls, hauled trash, and cleaned
toilets. After he turned sixteen, he worked on the extra gangs at the
Rock Island Railroad, laying and repairing tracks during long, hot
summer days, and during frigid Christmas breaks. He gave most of
the money he earned to his family to help buy school supplies,
clothes, and food for his nine brothers and sisters. Brother Tanilo
remembers, too, that Frank made his younger brothers slingshots,
and bought the family a bicycle they all used. "It was a big deal to

Frank Sandoval

have a bike," Tanilo said. "It wasn't his bike, it was all of ours bike. His things were our things. That's just how it was."

Unlike Joe, Frank didn't excel in school. He struggled with English, and McKinley Elementary held him back three times. But Frank proved to be a stubborn workhorse, and, unlike many of the boys from Little Mexico, Frank didn't quit school. When he graduated from East Moline High School at age twenty-one, he bought himself a new suit for graduation, using money he'd saved for years. "It was a big deal to have a suit to show that education meant something to you," Tanilo said. "Wearing the suit to graduation showed that you were an American." Then he gave the suit to his younger brothers Emilio and Tanilo to wear when they graduated.

Frank and Joe didn't like their family living without electricity, running water, and indoor plumbing. With their own money, they hired an electrician to bring power to the family home, and a plumber to bring running water and install toilets inside. They added flooring to the ground floor rooms where their mother and sisters slept. They bought their mother a washing machine. Before that, Angelina and her daughters hauled water from spigots on the other side of 2nd Street, then sat on the front lawn and washed huge loads of clothes — hard work, especially in winter. "Dad didn't mind living without electricity and plumbing, that's all he'd ever known in Mexico, but Joe and Frank wanted to do better. They wanted to make life easier for mom. They wanted to live like Americans, not Mexicans," Tanilo said.

While Joe married and fathered two children. Frank's family wasn't sure if he even had a girlfriend. Frank was very private, and his family didn't know what he did when he wasn't working or going to school. "There were rumors, but back then you didn't bring girls home," Tanilio, said. "You met them in secret at the movies or someplace. We don't know [if he had a girlfriend]. Mom didn't like any girls the boys brought home, or any of the boys the girls brought home." After graduating in 1942, Frank landed a job as a janitor at the Rock Island Arsenal, but the U.S. Army soon drafted him.

Frank was assigned to be a combat engineer, and his unit, Company C of the 209th Engineers Combat Battalion, trained in Texas,

Missouri, and California before shipping to the other side of the world to fight in a war he and his fellows engineers likely little understood. The Japanese had invaded China in June 1937, and subsequently captured China's seaports, effectively blocking import of food and war materials. In the first years of the war, the British used the Burma Road to ship supplies from India to China, but the Japanese cut the Burma Road in 1942, leaving treacherous airlifts over the Himalayas as the only method of supplying the Chinese. Frank and some seventeen thousand other American engineers and some eighty thousand Chinese, Indian, and Burmese were assigned to the task of building a new road through northern Burma — called the Ledo Road — that the Allies could use to reach China.

American Col. Charles Gleim called the proposed Ledo Road "the toughest engineering job on the planet." British Prime Minister Winston Churchill dismissed the proposed road as "an immense, laborious task, unlikely to be finished before the need for it had passed." Churchill added: "We argued that the enormous expenditure of manpower and material would not be worthwhile. But we never succeeded in deflecting the Americans from their purpose. Their national psychology is such that the bigger the idea, the more wholeheartedly and obstinately do they throw themselves into making it a success." Plans called for the engineers to build a 1,079-mile-long road — including seven hundred bridges — in an area where an average of 150 inches of rain fell every spring and summer. The road began at an elevation of five hundred feet in northeast India and climbed over ten thousand-foot passes on the Himalayan plateau, ending in Kunming. In addition to building the road, orders called for the engineers to install six pipelines for oil and gas along the road.

Charles Monroe, a fellow member of Frank's Company C of the 209th Engineers, recounted the unit's travels in a ten-page handwritten letter to Angelina Sandoval, dated August 20, 1985. The American engineers traveled by ship from New York to Rio de Janeiro, then around Cape Horn, and across the Pacific Ocean to India, arriving in Bombay on October 12, 1943. "That was the year the famine [in India] was so great," wrote Monroe. "We shared what food we could with them, but when they smelled the canned food and detected meat in it, they would throw it away. They . . . worship cattle. . . . The crackers and chocolate candy they liked." Monroe wrote that the American GIs crossed India on trains. ". . . [M]any, many times the train would have to stop to let someone remove a starving person from the tracks. . . .We moved at a snail's pace because some mountain areas were so steep the trains would hardly go." Frank's unit arrived at Ledo, India, and moved toward the India-Burma border via trucks. "The next day," Monroe wrote, "when we could really see the mountains and the road, it was scary because the road was so narrow and curves so sharp the truck had to back up to make the turn."

After arriving at the road project, Monroe said Frank drove one of the huge dump trucks and was "in charge of putting in culverts." They built bridges and cut a landing field for C-47 cargo planes. "Food was not always the best. Sometimes we would get fish from the river by using dynamite or a T.N.T. block — not a whole block but just enough to stun the fish so they would come to the top and we would pick them by the use of a boat. Many days for breakfast we would have powdered eggs and tomatoes cooked together. It was eat or do without." Frank's unit labored in a land where tigers hunted men, rogue elephants roamed, and Japanese snipers lurked. Disease — malaria, typhus, dysentery, jungle rot — and snipers claimed the lives of more than eleven hundred Americans working on the road. The Ledo Road cut through cliffs, enormous peaks, forests, and crossed rain-swollen rivers and streams. Up to fifteen inches of rain might fall in a single day during the monsoon season. Fifty-three percent of the U.S. troops in Burma came down with some high fever, usually caused by malaria. Theodore White wrote in *Time* magazine: "American engineers doctored sick work elephants with opium and paid native laborers with opium, too."

The Allies' strategy for fighting the war against the Axis called for the defeat of Germany to take priority over the conflict with Japan. As a result of this so-called Europe First policy, Allied forces in the China-Burma-India (CBI) Theater faced chronic supply shortages. The Ledo Road was to run through the Burmese town of Myitkyina, which the Japanese held. On May 17, 1944, an American

force popularly known as "Merrill's Marauders" (after its commander, Brig. Gen. Frank Merrill) captured the main airfield at
Myitkyina, and it looked like victory was in hand, but the Japanese
rushed in some five thousand troops and retained control of the
town and could not be dislodged. The ensuing Allied siege of Myitkyina featured clashes "as viciously concentrated as any battle in
World War II." At the end of May, U.S. Army General Joseph Stilwell, commander of Allied forces in north Burma, wrote his wife:
"This has been a knock-down-and-drag-out affair. . . . I felt guilty
about [the casualties]." In a diary entry he wrote: "I often dream of
going down into holes to pull the kids out, or looking for them
frantically under water. I think of situations . . . they turn my guts to
water." Daily rainfalls of up to fifteen inches hindered operations
and slowed or halted outright efforts to bring in reinforcements.
On one such day Stilwell wrote: "Rain — if we can't land planes we
can't land troops . . . this is just one of those terrible worry days
when you wish you were dead."

Allied troops — American, Chinese, and British — lacked food
and medical supplies, and illness forced the evacuation of seventy-
five to one hundred men every day. The troops that stayed were
almost too exhausted to fight, sometimes falling asleep during Japanese attacks. A desperate Stilwell ordered two battalions of engineers from the Ledo Road to Myitkyina. This meant Frank Sandoval
would go to one of the worst combat fronts in World War II. Though
nominally combat engineers, Frank and the road-builders "had not
held a rifle since basic training and initially proved worthless." Stilwell ordered basic training behind the lines for the 209th and 236th
Engineer Combat battalions. The engineers worked in three shifts
of eight hours each to prepare themselves for combat. Then Frank
and his fellow engineers shipped to the front. Monroe wrote: "At 4
A.M. the next day (May 24) we were told to get ready to load on the
planes and move into combat. . . .This was the most frightening
time we all experienced while in the service. When we landed in
Myitkyina it was a gravel airfield . . . . When we were told to move
toward the front lines, no one wanted to move, because we could
hear the guns. We knew this was not a training mission, but the real

thing. It was more jungle, rain and mud." Another engineer, Lloyd L. Kessler, wrote in the March 2001 issue of *World War II* magazine: "As we circled the field at Myitkyina, bullets pinged off our fuselage like hail on a tin roof. On the ground, chaos reigned. Officers shouted orders at confused soldiers, airplanes landed and took off at a ferocious rate and Japanese snipers fired at us from a distance." One American commander said the engineers were marginally useless when they first arrived at the front. "They are in many cases simply terrified."

Frank's unit and the 236th Combat Engineers were attached to Merrill's decimated force to create a provisional regiment that dug in on Myitkyina's northern approaches. In early June, the regiment crossed through enemy lines and then attacked the Myitkyina airport from the north. Kessler remembered:

> Our first major offensive could properly be called a failure. We were ordered to neutralize a 75mm gun emplacement that was creating havoc among the Chinese troops that were supporting us. Reconnaissance told us that a platoon of Japanese soldiers stood between us and the gun. Since it was almost dark, we decided to wait until dawn before trying to seize the position. . . . Whatever sleep we might have gotten was interrupted at 2300 hours by a volley of rifle fire. Orange tracers cut through the darkness. One of our machine guns opened up, answered by the rapid chatter of a Japanese light machine gun. Flares bathed the area in bright light. I saw the Japanese coming toward us — silently, not a banzai attack but slowly and deliberately, as though they expected little opposition. I held my rifle with the sling wrapped around my arm . . . knelt and waited until I saw them clearly. I started firing and kept firing until there were no more Japanese in front of me. They stopped shooting flares. I stared into the darkness, but all I could see or hear was the whimpering and groaning of the wounded. . . . At dawn the enemy decided to kill us from a distance. A big artillery piece opened up. I heard a rush of air as some-

thing big whizzed past me, then a loud explosion somewhere behind me. They had not found the range yet. Despite this bit of good fortune, we knew we were outgunned
and outnumbered, and the decision was made to retreat.[14]

Frank Sandoval, Lloyd Kessler, and other surviving engineers
and Marauders fled back through enemy lines and returned to
Allied positions on June 16. His unit dug in along the banks of the
monsoon-swollen Irrawaddy River, using foxholes previously dug by
Japanese soldiers. On June 26, 1944, the Japanese attacked across
the river. Mortar shells landed amid the engineers and Marauders.
"The Japanese 50mm grenade launcher, commonly called a knee
mortar, had a range of 700 yards, far beyond what was needed to an-
nihilate us," Kessler wrote. Then Japanese rifles and machine guns
began firing. Engineers and Marauders fell — including Sandoval.

"Frank was killed in action and suffered no agony, as he was
killed by enemy gun fire on an attack. Please do not picture the
worst, for he went quickly, perhaps not knowing it," wrote Pastor
Thurman H. Tobias, the division chaplain, in a letter to Angelina
and Eduviges. Fellow engineers dug a grave for Frank near the
Irrawaddy River. A friend cut bamboo and made a cross. Engineers
and Marauders lowered Frank's body into the grave, shoveled dirt
back in and planted the cross. His dog tags and helmet were placed
on the cross to mark the grave. As the engineers and Marauders
crouched on their knees and bellies around Frank's grave — and as
bullets flew overhead and mortars exploded nearby — Tobias hur-
riedly read St. John 14:1–8:

> Let not your heart be troubled: ye believe in God, believe
>   also in me.
> In my Father's House are many mansions: if it were not so,
>   I would have told you.
> I go to prepare a place for you.
> And if I go to prepare a place for you, I will come again
>   and receive you into
> myself; that where I am, there ye may be also.

And whither I go ye know, and the way ye know.
Thomas saith unto him, Lord, we know not whither thou
    goest; and how can we know the way?
Jesus said unto him, I am the way, the truth, and the life:
    no man cometh unto the Father, but by me.
If ye know me, ye should have known my Father also: and
    from henceforth ye know him, and have seen him.

There was, Tobias wrote Frank's family, "little time for ceremony, as enemy fire was all about us." Monroe's letter to Angelina said: "This is the most difficult part of this letter. I know we left several members of our 209th Engineers Battalion buried in Burma in God's good earth, not to be forgotten, but to be remembered as we loved them and why they died."

The seventy-seven–day siege of Myitkyina lasted until August 3, 1944, when the Japanese commander ordered his troops to retreat. He then took out his pistol, put it to his head, and pulled the trigger. Many Japanese troops also committed suicide. Overall, approximately nine hundred enemy soldiers died in the battle. The 209th Combat Engineers suffered 71 men killed and 179 wounded. In total, the siege at Myitkyina claimed six hundred Allied soldiers killed and eleven hundred wounded. Frank's company was awarded a Presidential Unit Citation, and the army sent his parents a Purple Heart, which his sister, Georgia Sandoval Herrera, treasures.

After the battle, soldiers recovered Frank's body from his shallow grave near the Irrawaddy River, and reburied him in a U.S. military cemetery in India. In 1949, the army disinterred Frank's body again and shipped it back to Silvis. The army buried him with full military honors in the National Military Cemetery at the Rock Island Arsenal, next to his brother, Joseph.

CHAPTER EIGHT

One Family per Stall

A chicken in every pot and a car in every garage.
—Herbert Hoover campaign slogan in 1928

In the spring of 1937, at the nadir of the Great Depression, Joseph Sandoval spent his last dollar. He couldn't find a job, buy food, or pay rent. The landlady said she didn't want her house torn up by a dozen Mexican kids—Joseph's nine boys and three girls—at least not without rent. "Get out!" said the landlady, adding that if they didn't leave voluntarily the sheriff would forcibly put them on the street. The Depression had plunged the Rock Island Railroad—Sandoval's employer—into a death spiral. Although the railroad had cut employees' pay by 10 percent, shuttered stations, and stopped fixing tracks and bridges it still couldn't pay its bills. The railroad filed for bankruptcy protection on June 7, 1933, and then eliminated Sandoval's job. He could find no other employment, and hunger and cold crept into his home. In desperation, he gave away his youngest son.

Sandoval—and millions of others—desperately looked for work. He found some for a time at a steel mill fifty miles away in Sterling. When that mill closed, he found sporadic employment with the federal government's Works Progress Administration, but the state of Illinois passed a law barring non-U.S. citizens from holding government jobs, and Sandoval, a Mexican citizen who fled to the United States in 1917, was fired. That meant his children, all American citizens, would go hungry.

The Deportation Act of 1929 made it easier for public officials to deport "aliens of any race" for a variety of reasons. Many Mexicans didn't apply for relief programs to avoid exposure to authorities and possible deportation. Even when they tried, relief agencies were reluctant to give food to Mexican men, saying relief should go first to Americans. Some local governments urged forced repatriation of Mexicans as a means of reducing unemployment and demands on public relief. Mexicans fled to the shadows.

On good days, Joseph's children took unwrapped bean sandwiches to school. When there was no food in the house, son Al Sandoval said, "I'd tell my teacher I'd lost my lunch, and the teacher would ask, 'Who's got some lunch to share with Al?' and I'd eat some really good food." His sister, Rufina Sandoval, added: "I was about ten years old and fifteen pounds underweight, so the school nurse pulled me out of class to give me a glass of milk and a graham cracker. Milk was a real treat. We all were raised on coffee because dad could never afford milk." Rufina had two skirts and one pair of shoes to wear to school. The boys shared hard-worn hand-me-downs. "Dad repaired shoes for the whole street. Sometimes he just used cardboard to make new soles," she said. "We just didn't have nothing." Willie Sandoval, at twelve, the second oldest child in the family, took a job as a janitor at McKinley School, with all his pay going to help feed the family.

After their landlady evicted the Sandovals in May 1937, the family moved into the basement of their Aunt Constance's boarding house in nearby East Moline. With too many mouths to feed and no income, Joseph Sandoval "gave" his youngest child, baby Fred, to Fred's godparents, a childless couple. Sandoval heard about sugar beet farmers in northern Iowa who needed help with harvests, and he contracted with a farmer to bring in that year's crop. Needing field hands, Sandoval pulled his children out of school. All members of the family would help, but the heart of his harvest crew would be his oldest children—Rueben, fifteen; Willie, thirteen; Rufina, twelve; and Harry, eleven. Aunt Constance drove them to the sugar beet farm about ten miles from Clarion, Iowa. "We all piled in her big, old car—I think it was a Pontiac. We sat on top of each other and stuffed our things wherever we could," said Rufina. "When we got to a rest stop, someone watched us get out in amazement and asked: 'How many more people do you have in there?' " Counting Aunt Constance, there were fourteen—but they were all skinny, perhaps even malnourished. Their possessions were a few boxes of clothes, several blankets, a couple of dollars loaned them by Aunt Connie, and some tortillas, beans and potatoes given by friends from 2nd Street.

The farmer provided the family with a tiny old trailer, and a covered wagon. "It was like we were pioneers crossing the prairie in a Conestoga wagon, except we weren't going anywhere," Rufina remembered sixty-eight years later. "We ate eggs, beans, and potatoes one night and the next night we ate potatoes, beans, and eggs. The next night, for variety, we'd eat beans, eggs, and potatoes. We never ate meat—except if the boys caught a bird." The boys supplemented the family's diet by hunting pigeons, pheasants, and any other birds they could snare. "We'd search the old barns and catch the pigeons and eat them that night," Al Sandoval said. "We also hunted pheasants in the fields by sneaking up on them real slowly." The boys, Rufina said, would camouflage themselves with tree branches and creep along the ground. "It was fun," Al said, "but mostly it was trying to have something to eat." Rufina added: "We didn't roast the birds, we used them for soup to make the food go further."

Joseph and his two oldest sons, Rueben and Willie, rose at first light, about 5:00 A.M., to work the sugar beet fields. At about 7:00 A.M., they returned for breakfast, after which the mother and the rest of the older children—all but the very youngest—also went to work thinning and weeding around the sugar beets. The long hours in the hot, humid fields took their toll. Temperatures climbed to nearly one hundred degrees, and the humidity reached over 90 percent. They didn't always have easy access to water. Eleven-year-old Harry lost his ability to walk — "because of rheumatism, that's what we called it. We don't know what it was — he just couldn't walk. We didn't have any doctor or hospital," said Rufina. But every hand was needed, no matter if the legs were unable. So older brothers Willie and Ruben carried Harry to the fields each morning. "Harry couldn't walk but he still had to work," said Rufina. "We all worked on our knees all day anyway, so once he (Harry) got to the field, he just crawled around on his knees. We just couldn't afford to not have him work. We thinned the rows, then we weeded. We'd look up and we couldn't even see the end of the rows. We wouldn't come in until after 9:00 P.M." Then, in the dark, Willie and Rueben carried Harry back to the wagon for soup and sleep and another day working in the field.

The farmer gave the Sandovals burlap gunnysacks, which they filled with straw and used as mattresses. "Only two or three people could sleep in the trailer because it was so small," brother Ruben said. "The rest of us slept in the open. We didn't have a roof over our heads." While the sugar beet crop ripened, Joseph Sandoval took his family into southern Minnesota to harvest onions. The family — and other Mexican and Mexican American families — shared a barn. The owners assigned each family to a stall. "We lived where the horses and cows had lived. We lived like animals," Rufina said. After harvesting the onions, the family went back to the sugar beet farm, to finish the harvest and get paid. The family saved every penny. "Dad taught us how to save — it was survival," said Rufina. "We didn't spend anything on anything unless we absolutely had to."

At the end of the harvest, the family returned to Silvis, and Joseph Sandoval bought — for $900 earned that summer — a ramshackle two-story wood-frame house at 214 2nd Street in Silvis near the southern end of the street. "Dad was so proud to finally own a home of his own," said his son, Al. "I remember waking up on a winter morning and finding a line of snow on the bed. There were so many cracks in the siding that the wind drove snow through them. We stuffed the cracks with newspapers. But we didn't care, we had a roof over our heads and no landlady who could evict us." Rufina added: "The birds could fly in and out of the house, the cracks were so big." The house's main floor was dirt. A pot-bellied stove on the first floor served for heat and cooking. The house had no electricity, running water or indoor plumbing. Upstairs were two bedrooms. There was little bedding and few blankets. The family slept three and four to a bed, and brothers Rueben, Willie, and Harry (who'd regained his ability to walk without medical attention) shared a bed. "They were each other's blankets," Al said. Joseph Sandoval got some work with the still-bankrupt Rock Island, then got a job with a new ordnance plant in Iowa.

Then tragedy struck. Joseph's wife, Carmen Sandoval, who had already given birth to twelve children, gave birth to twins—John and Peter—on September 1, 1939. But the twins lived only hours, and Willie and Rufina watched a Roman Catholic priest baptize and then give last rites to them. Three days after the twins died, their mother died of complications of childbirth. Carmen Sandoval was thirty-even. The family buried her in St. Mary's Cemetery, but couldn't afford a marker for her grave. "She was born to a wealthy family (in Mexico)," said Rufina. "Her family had maids, so she'd never learned how to cook or clean. Then she came to America and had all these children, and faced all the poverty. She learned how to cook and clean and make do. We all loved her so much." Rufina—the oldest female in the family—dropped out of school to run the household. "I had all these kids to feed and take care of," she said. "It was a lot of work for a fourteen-year-old."

Back in Silvis, Willie and Rueben resumed boxing, Rueben fighting at 112 pounds, Willie at 118. "Lots of us thought boxing could be a way out [of poverty]," Al Sandoval said. But it was a steep climb. When Willie, then seventeen, won a big fight in 1941, the *Moline Dispatch* wrote about how the Anglo kid lost, not how Willie won: "Young Billy Russell, who scaled to the top of the Quad-City flyweights . . . fell off his high perch as a leading contender with a reverberating crash Tuesday night when he dropped a close decision to Willie Sandoval, finalist in the 1940 Golden Gloves." After

Willie Sandoval

graduating from East Moline High in 1941, Willie went to work with his father at the Bettendorf Ordnance Steel Foundry, located just across the Mississippi River in Iowa.

Willie had a serious girlfriend, a high school diploma, a strong constitution, and a good work ethic. Compared with the poverty during the Great Depression, Willie's prospects were excellent— until the Japanese struck Pearl Harbor. Willie, eighteen and consumed with patriotism, volunteered for the U.S. Army. His efforts to get in the air force failed, but his great physical condition as a boxer helped get him into paratrooper training. On June 25, 1943, after accelerated training, Willie graduated from jump school and became a paratrooper—dangerous, elite duty that earned extra pay. He sent his first paycheck home to buy a monument for his mother's unmarked grave. In July, he came home on leave for a short visit. He looked splendid in uniform, and all the young boys wanted their photos taken with him. He left on a train for Fort Benning, Georgia, on July 3, 1943.

The army assigned Willie to F Company of the 504th Regiment of the 82nd Airborne Division, and sent his unit across the Atlantic to French Morocco, landing at Oran. One paratrooper, James Megellas, wrote in his memoir: "Most women were veiled, and for the first time we were exposed to a different culture, language, dress and behavior. All of the immorality that accompanies the savagery of war in the war zone was prevalent. Pimps and prostitutes were hawking their wares." Willie and his fellow paratroopers traveled by train housed in boxcars not unlike the boxcar in which Willie was born in 1924: their destination was the Allies' airborne training center in Oujda, in northeast Morocco near the Algerian border. Megellas described the training center as "rows of tents in a barren, desolate area devoid of vegetation or shade." The town of Oujda was a primitive place of unpaved streets lined with horse-drawn carriages but no automobiles. The paratroopers slept in tents without cots or electricity and drew water from a well for washing and shaving. Their training ended abruptly when an American army faced disaster.

The Allies landed on the Italian mainland on September 3,

1943, and the fascist Italian government surrendered on September 8. The next day, the American Fifth Army under Gen. Mark Clark landed at Salerno. Allied victory in Italy seemed imminent. But the Germans counterattacked fiercely, pinning Clark's troops to within just six hundred yards of the landing beaches. The Fifth Army was in danger of being pushed into the sea.

Clark sent an order to Gen. Matthew Ridgway, commander of the U.S. 82nd Airborne Division, saying: "The fighting on Salerno has taken a turn for the worse, and the situation is touch and go. I realize the time normally needed to prepare for a drop, but this is an exception. I want you to make a drop within our lines on the beachhead, and I want you to make it tonight. This is a must!" Ridgway in turn ordered Col. Rueben Tucker's 504th Parachute Infantry Regiment, including Willie's unit, to jump that very night. Willie and the other paratroopers scrambled to the parachute shed at Oujda on September 13, and loaded into waiting planes. "Men, here's the poop," one platoon leader said. "Those . . . Krauts are kicking the hell out of our straight-legs [army infantrymen] over at Salerno. Mark Clark wants us to rescue his boys. When the green light comes on, jump. When you hit the ground, be ready for anything. We're supposed to drop behind our own lines — but the Krauts might be on the DZ (drop zone) when we get there. Any questions?"

Just ten hours after Clark wrote his "this is a must" order, Willie Sandoval and the rest of the paratroopers of the 504th Regiment took off in the desperate effort to save the U.S. Fifth Army. At 3:00 A.M. on September 14 — two days before his twentieth birthday — Willie made his first combat jump just six hundred feet above the ground. The thirteen hundred paratroopers of the 504th landed in the midst of the Fifth Army. "Word that 1,300 tough American paratroopers had leaped onto the battlefield, like lightening from the black sky, infected haggard and demoralized men with a new sense of confidence, even courage," wrote one historian.

Willie spent his twentieth birthday, September 16, 1943, under constant artillery bombardment. The next day, the 504th helped beat back the last major attack by the Germans on the Salerno beachhead. Thirty paratroopers were killed, 150 wounded, and one was reported missing in action. Allied casualties in the invasion totaled more than thirteen thousand, including 2,149 men killed, but the "Allies emerged from the blood and sand with an unshakable foothold on the road to Rome." The German Tenth Army withdrew on September 18. General Clark wrote: "Remarkable courage and sacrifice by every American and British soldier on the beachhead helped with this victory. But it had been touch and go all the way. When victory or defeat hung in the balance, the 82nd Airborne reinforcement drops . . . tilted the scales in our favor."

On October 1, Allied forces entered Naples, the first major European city to fall to the Allies in World War II. Willie's unit remained on the ground and moved north, part of the Allies' slow advance toward Rome. His unit fought in October in the Naples and Foggia area, suffering heavy casualties, until it was finally relieved on November 23, 1943.

After celebrating Thanksgiving, Willie and the rest of the 504th relieved the 3rd U.S. Ranger Battalion on Hill 950, high in the snowy Apennine Mountains. Headquarters ordered the unit to climb ice-coated, 3,950-foot Mount Sammucro. Finding the ground too rocky for digging foxholes, the paratroopers sought cover behind boulders while taking fire from German snipers, mortars, and artillery. The ground was so steep and the paths so narrow that all supplies were brought in — and all bodies taken out — on the backs of mules and donkeys. Chaplain Delbert Kuehl described the scene as "pure misery up there. We will never forget those long days and nights, week after week, in the rain and snow, not enough to eat and the constant shelling in the Italian mountains." Willie ate K Rations — compressed meat or eggs, hard biscuits, processed cheese, gum, and candy. K Rations were intended as a single day's ration, not as a steady diet. Still, it was better chow than he ate in the Iowa sugar beet fields during the Depression. Each soldier got one canteen of water a day for drinking, making coffee, brushing teeth, and washing themselves. They melted snow for extra water.

They celebrated Christmas in the combat zone. "Christmas Eve night at the front was calm, cold and serene," recalled Megellas. "As I strained to hear the voices between artillery shells, I clearly recognized the carols Silent Night and Oh Come, All Ye Faithful. . . . Christmas services were behind us proclaiming the birth of the Savior, and Germans were in front of us; like us, they had one purpose — kill their fellow man." Christmas Day was wet and cold and there was constant shelling by both sides. Willie's unit was relieved on December 27, 1943, and sent to liberated Naples for rest and relaxation. During nineteen days at the mountainous front, Willie's unit suffered 54 killed, 226 wounded, and two missing in action.

After Naples, Willie's unit made an amphibious landing with the aim of blocking road and rail traffic between Rome and Anzio, and ultimately freeing Nazi-occupied Rome. On January 22, 1944, Willie's unit, carried in thirteen amphibious craft, landed at Red Beach near Anzio, some forty miles south of Rome. The surprised Germans regrouped and tried to drive the Allies into the sea with heavy artillery, and hand-to-hand infantry fighting. Willie and the other American paratroopers fought bitterly along the Mussolini Canal. For more than eight weeks they fought from foxholes much like the trench warfare of World War I. The war along the Canale Mussolini was brutal and deadly, as Germans atop Colli Lazuali, a nearby steep mountain, could observe nearly every movement of Willie's unit. Troopers suffered in waterlogged, frigid, cramped holes while buffeted by thick sheets of rain and howling winds. Artillery and mortar shells fell on paratroopers huddled helplessly in holes. During this campaign, the 504th earned its famed nickname, "Devils in baggy pants." Allied soldiers found this entry in the diary of a German officer killed at Anzio: "American parachutists — devils in baggy pants — are less than 100 meters from my outpost line. I can't sleep at night; they pop up from nowhere and we never know when or how they will strike next. Seems like the black-hearted devils are everywhere."

Amid this horror, on March 4, 1944, Willie wrote his father "from Italy on Italian stationery," and said he couldn't wait to return home "where you can step out from your doorstep and admire the sunshine and fresh air instead of fearing gun shells, air attacks and breathe the smoke of gun powder. When I step into the door-step and say 'I'm home Dad' that will be the happiest day of my life."

Willie and the 504th spent 151 days on the front lines in Italy — including sixty-two days fighting for the Mussolini Canal — before being relieved on March 23, 1944. During Anzio battle, Willie's regiment lost 120 men killed, 410 wounded and sixty missing in action. Overall the Allies suffered more than thirty thousand casualties, including forty-four hundred killed. In his memoirs, Megellas wrote: "The 504th had more men killed in 62 days in combat on the Anzio beach than in any other campaign we fought, including the parachute jumps in Holland (Market-Garden) and the Battle of the Bulge. The 504th received the Presidential Unit Citation for meritorious contributions to the war effort.

In April 1944, Willie's unit was withdrawn from Italy and shipped on the *Capetown Castle* to Liverpool, England, to rejoin the 82nd Airborne Division. Army command decided the 504th was too depleted to help in the upcoming invasion of Normandy, so the unit stayed in Leicester for rest, relaxation, reorganization, and to absorb reinforcements. U.S. Gen. Dwight D. Eisenhower, the Supreme Allied Commander, inspected the 504th and told them: "You men have accomplished great things and I have greater things in store for you."

In a three-month period following the Normandy landings (on June 6, 1994) the Western Allies liberated France and advanced all the way to the German border. At the same time, in the east, Soviet forces scored spectacular victories and were driving inexorably toward the enemy's homeland. By early autumn Germany's armed forces, reeling with defeat and weakened by enormous losses in men and matériel, seemed on the brink of collapse. An intelligence summary written for the British Second Army on September 5, 1944, noted: "[It] is tolerably certain that the enemy has not kept at home a reserve which is well enough trained or equipped to hold an invading force at bay for long" General George S. Patton, commander of the U.S. Third Army, said his army could go through the Siegfried Line "like shit through a goose." An aide to Gen. Omar N. Bradley, commander of the U.S. 12th Army Group and Patton's boss, wrote on September 15: "Brad and Patton agree neither will be too surprised if we are on the Rhine in a week." The common hope was the war would soon be over, and the boys would be coming home for Christmas.

British Field Marshal Bernard L. Montgomery, commander of the 21st Army Group, convinced Eisenhower that the war could be significantly shortened by outflanking the Siegfried Line with a narrow thrust across the lower Rhine through Holland to the Ruhr, Germany's industrial heartland. Codenamed Operation Market-Garden, Montgomery's offensive would be conducted by the First Airborne Army and the British XXX Corps, a powerful armored force: the airborne units, dropping as far sixty miles behind enemy lines in Holland, would seize and hold bridges on a series of rivers for British tanks to use on what was meant to be a swift advance into northern Germany. En route the British would achieve another key objective: clearing V-2 missile-launching sites from the Dutch coast and thus end attacks by these revolutionary new weapons on London. The offensive was to start on September 17.

Willie's unit spent September 16, 1944, in a fog-shrouded, rain-drenched tent at Spanhoe airfield in rural central England. On the eve of what was to be history's largest airborne offensive, Willie and his buddies wrote letters home, and updated their wills. It was Willie's twenty-first birthday.

On Sunday, September 17, 2,023 troop transport planes and 478 gliders took off from twenty-four airfields in England. Escorted by more than eleven hundred fighter planes flying about fifteen hundred feet above the ground, the armada carried forty-five thousand men — twenty thousand paratroopers, fifteen thousand glider soldiers and ten thousand infantrymen. Five hours after taking off, the airborne force completed its daring daylight drop in Holland with fewer than 2 percent casualties. The 504th dropped south of Nijmegen with orders to capture the highway bridge over the Waal River at Nijmegen. American and British soldiers, supported by British tanks, fought a fierce street-by-street battle through the mostly residential southern part of Nijmegen to reach the edge of

Hunter Park, just four hundred yards from the bridge. The park was "congested with SS troops concealed in air-raid shelters and huddled in foxholes and trenches." The Allied commander, American Gen. James Gavin, decided to attack both ends of the bridge simultaneously, so a battalion of Rube Tucker's 504th Regiment was ordered to cross the five hundred-yard-wide Waal two miles downstream in hand-paddled boats. "I remember we all looked at each other and said this was a suicide mission if we had ever seen one," said Capt. Delbert Kuehl, the regiment's Protestant chaplain. The paratroopers climbed into twenty-five British boats that were nineteen feet long with canvas sides and flat plywood bottoms. Eight canoe paddles were supposed to be in each boat, but not all had the requisite number. The river current was eight miles an hour. Thirteen paratroopers were assigned to each little boat. Willie's unit, Company F, stayed on the south bank of the river to provide covering fire. Willie's unit stretched out in exposed positions on the south shore and blistered the north bank with automatic weapons and rifle fire. There were few reserves, as bad weather had forced postponement of parachute drops to reinforce the Allies at Nijmegen and the beleaguered British paratroopers at nearby Arnhem, which faced disaster.

Time was running short (especially at Arnhem) so the 504th was ordered to cross the river — in broad daylight. On the river, wrote Megellas, "bullets were flying so thick and fast that they gave a reasonable facsimile of a steel curtain. By now the surface of the Waal was covered with our small canvas crafts and crammed with frantically paddling men. Defenseless, frail, canvas boats jammed to overflowing with humanity, all striving desperately to get across the Waal as quickly as possible. Large numbers of men were being hit in all boats, and the bottoms of these crafts were littered with the wounded and dead. . . . But at last we reached the other side. We climbed over the dead and wounded in the bottom of the boat and up to our knees in water waded to shore where behind a small embankment we flopped down gasping for breath, safe for the moment from the incessant firing."

Kuehl remembered that only eleven or twelve of the twenty-five boats made it across the river. At 4:45 P.M., Col. Rueben Tucker, the 504th's commander, radioed a message: "Regiment across the river. Advancing toward bridge." An hour or so later, Tucker reported capturing the north end of the bridge. But Germans still controlled the south end.

Major Benjamin Vandervoort, commanding the Americans at the south end of the bridge, was then ordered to attack. Historian William B. Breuer described the action: "There was no tactical plan, no time for flanking maneuvers and decoy operations. Rather two companies of paratroopers and . . . tanks would simply rush the bridge. . . . Just before 6 p.m., under the cover of a blistering fusillade of fire from troopers in second-story windows, 280 All-Americans, along with Churchill tanks — four abreast — charged the German positions, shooting and yelling. This was the moment of truth. Should Vandervoort's men fail, Market-Garden would fail — and Rube Tucker's Five-O-Fours would be cut off on the German side of the Waal."

Willie's unit rushed to the south end of the bridge. Willie and some 280 other paratroopers followed tanks and charged the German positions, manned by crack SS troops. "Tanks rolled over foxholes and trenches, grinding SS men into pulp, and fired point-blank into air raid shelters. . . . It was a fight to the death, dog-eat-dog, a bloody clash of elite adversaries — SS troops against American paratroopers supported by British tanks. In the slaughterhouse, men on both sides became crazed."

Vandervoort recalled: "No quarter was asked by either side and none was given. The fight was so close and intense that individual Germans were either too brave or too scared to surrender. They seemed indifferent to death. Our paratroopers reacted with ice-cold ruthlessness. . . . Finally, the SS troops broke, and those who could, ran east and west and some actually jumped into the Waal River. Thirty minutes after the jump-off, resistance at the south end of the bridge had been neutralized." Last-minute German efforts to blow up the fifteen hundred-foot bridge failed.

The victory proved hollow. Inexplicably to the Americans, the British tanks halted at the Nijmegen bridge rather than advancing to help the beleaguered British paratroopers besieged in Arnhem. The tanks waited eighteen hours for infantry support to catch up with the tanks before advancing. Tucker later wrote: "We had killed ourselves crossing the Waal to grab the north end of the bridge. We just stood there, seething, as the British settled in for the night, failing to take advantage of the situation. We couldn't understand it. It simply wasn't the way we did things in the American army— especially if it had been our guys hanging by their fingernails eleven miles away."

Three hours before the Allied tanks and troops crossed the Waal, German tanks had retaken the Arnhem bridge, the "bridge too far." Had the tanks and troops of XXX Corps reached Arnhem while the British paratroopers still held the bridge, Montgomery's plan might have succeeded. Instead, only a mixed force of some five hundred Allied paratroopers, mostly British, reached the bridge at Arnhem. German Capt. Karl Godau later recorded: "Their attack could have worked. We had so little. If they had kept coming that night, there was nothing worth mentioning between their halting place and Eindhoven [just outside Arnhem]."

Montgomery's plan failed, in part, because intelligence failed to detect the extensive presence of German troops and tanks, and because communications failures blindfolded commanders. Weather problems delayed reinforcements and re-supply efforts. One historian called Market-Garden "a rotten plan, poorly executed." Casualties exceeded seventeen thousand. British forces suffered 13,226 wounded or killed, and American losses were put at 3,974. The 82nd Airborne Division lost some two hundred men killed and seven hundred wounded in the offensive.

With the offensive halted, Willie and his fellow paratroopers hunkered down in foxholes on a defensive line extending 140 miles along the Dutch-German border. Worse than manning foxholes was night patrol. "If there is one thing a dogface hated, it was going out on night patrol behind enemy lines to capture prisoners," wrote Megellas; "[O]ne who has never been out on a combat patrol at night behind enemy lines could not possibly understand the eerie feeling the men had."

As darkness fell on Friday, October 6, 1944, Willie Sandoval's G Company patrol moved forward into the dense, gloomy woods of Thorensche Molen, in eastern Holland, just yards from the German border. Regimental command wanted the 82nd Airborne Division's northern flank moved to straighten the Allied line. The paratroopers were told that they would encounter only light resistance, but within ten minutes they were pinned down by machine-gun, rifle, and mortar fire. Firing in retaliation, American artillery bombarded German positions for an hour, setting the woods on fire. Smoke billowed, trees blazed, heat seared the skin — a scene out of Hades. Then the patrol, still under heavy fire, moved forward toward the border. The Germans, defending the borders of the Fatherland, fought desperately, and beat back a flanking patrol from another company, leaving Willie's unit isolated behind enemy lines.

At 11:15 P.M., the Germans shot an amber flare into the air. The Germans spotted Willie's patrol. Heavy German machine guns opened fire. The paratroopers ran east onto German soil. While climbing a fence, Willie was hit. He fell but the patrol ran on, leaving Willie in the blazing woods as the amber flare burned out. The unit's October 7 log read: "0115. Lt. Hanna's platoon still pinned down. Major Cook orders Lt. Hanna to withdraw when it is safe. Capt. Thomas, G Company, reports two men slightly wounded and one missing."

The army never recovered Willie's body. He was listed as missing in action for one year, until other members of the patrol confirmed seeing Willie shot atop the fence in the firefight in the eerie light of a German flare. The army listed Willie Sandoval's place of death as just east of the Dutch border in Zyffich, Germany. "Willie was a fighter," said his brother Al. "The country never gave him much as a kid, but he gave his country everything. I think he would be proud of how we all turned out. Most of us [Mexican Americans from 2nd Street] ended up leading good lives — lives we couldn't have had in

Mexico. America is the land of opportunity. America is worth fighting for — dying for. I think my brother would have agreed."

Joseph Sandoval hated that his son's body was never recovered and given a Christian burial. Many years later, his son Oscar traveled to the battle scene and posed for a photo next to the grave of an American soldier. Oscar told his father the grave was Willie's. Only then did Joseph Sandoval acknowledge his son's death. But after Joseph Sandoval died, Oscar admitted to his family that the grave he posed next to was not Willie's. Oscar admitted to faking the grave photo to ease his father's mind. Willie Sandoval remained one of over twenty thousand Americans whose bodies were never recovered from Europe's World War II battlefields.

CHAPTER NINE

Little Hands

Defend . . . to the last.
— German Generalleutnant Fritz Bayerlein's orders to his
troops on January 15, 1945, during the Battle of Bulge

On a hot, humid night in July, near midnight, Claro Solis waited
outside the gates of the John Deere Co. spreader plant in East
Moline, ready to resume battle. His foe had challenged him the
night before, perhaps even bested him and, worse still, laughed at
him. His foe did that too often, and with devastating effect. But
tonight, under the moon and stars outside the farm implement
plant along the Mississippi River, Claro soughtrevenge — and honor
for his sacred cause, and retribution for the laughter.

He had thought about revenge on the way to work and all
during his shift. He had been slow, tired, and even weak during last
night's battle. Tonight, he would be the first to strike, and his blows
would be deadly — and artful. Then, out of the plant gate, walked
his foe — Antonio — and the great battle resumed. But this was no
street knife fight between macho young men, perhaps fighting over
a woman or some perceived slight. No, this was more important.
After nine hard, sweaty hours of work during the plant's second

shift, Claro and Antonio faced a two-mile walk through the shabby industrial town back to Silvis's Little Mexico. The moon, stars, and lights from a few small taverns offered dim light. The streets were mostly deserted, but the few passersby would have been stunned had they understood what Claro and Antonio were fighting about in a passionate mixture of English and Spanish. They were brothers — sons of illiterate Mexican refugees — and they fought non-stop about the relative merits, values, and power of art versus music. Antonio defended music; Claro pleaded the cause of art.

"We settled this yesterday," Antonio said. "Music touches the soul. Music makes people sing and dance and want to make love. Everyone can sing, even if they don't know how bad they sound. Few people can or even want to paint and draw." Music, Antonio told his little brother, meant much to many people, while art meant much to few. His argument sent Claro into a frenzy. Art carried God's messages, Claro argued, and was much more important than music. Music was common, could even be heathen. People sang — usually badly — when they were drunk and foolish. Art, on the other hand, was the gift of God and the angels. Just look at the art in the church — art was how God shared beauty with his human creations. Tony laughed at Claro's naiveté — he was such a lover of God and goodness. Claro retorted that Tony just liked to play guitar to impress the girls. The argument didn't end when they reached home on 2nd Street. Their parents and sister were sleeping in the back of the house, so the brothers pulled out a chess set on the porch and moved their pieces by moonlight. And their argument about art versus music went on until dawn, and resumed every day and night until the brothers went to war. Many years later, when Tony was in his eighties, he told the author he hoped to resume the debate with Claro someday soon in heaven.

While most of the boys on 2nd Street boxed, Claro dabbled with watercolors and pencil-sketched self-portraits. The others struggled through classes, but Claro excelled at school and sought extra credit. The other boys chased girls — Claro remained chaste. Practicing their religion was a chore for many of the boys, but Claro loved the Roman Catholic Church, reciting the rosary, and high mass celebrated in

Claro Solis

Latin by their Polish priests. While the other boys climbed to the top of the neighborhood's great hill and sang and drank beer, Claro spent his late nights playing chess with Antonio debating the virtues and vices of humanity. He was perhaps the most unusual, certainly the most artistic, child born in the Silvis boxcars.

Midwives helped Manuela Solis deliver Claro — her fourth child — in the family's boxcar on August 12, 1920. Manuela and Gambino Solis married in a fifteenth-century Catholic church in poverty-stricken Barrio San Miguel in Leon, Guanajuato, just before the outbreak of the Mexican Revolution. Their first child — Claro's oldest brother, Augusto — was born in Leon, but when revolutionary armies swept through the nation drafting and shooting men, Gambino fled to the United States. For seven years, Manuela heard nothing of or from Gambino. Then, in 1917, after the worst of the revolution ended, Gabino returned to Mexico and took Manuela and Augusto to Texas, where their second son, Antonio, was born. Then the family moved to Silvis where Claro was conceived and born. He was baptized Joseph Claro Solis on August 21, 1921, at St. Mary's Catholic Church in East Moline.

His hard-working and hard-drinking father, Gambino, belittled Claro's artistic ambitions. He derisively called his son "Little Hands" because Claro avoided menial chores that might damage his hands and painting skills. Grudgingly, Claro swung hammers to drive spikes into rail lines, set pins at Andy's Bowling Alley in Moline, harvested onions in the fields just across the Mississippi River, and pulled weeds in the family garden. He pushed a broom and scrubbed toilets when his father got him a janitor's job. Claro did those jobs, but he wanted better. Claro believed his "little hands" were his ticket to a better life. His hands, he believed, would make him an artist and a successful American. He'd show that his father was wrong.

Claro had to grow up fast. The husband of his older sister, Kay, was struck by a train and killed while rushing through the train yard to a wedding reception. Claro — though still a teenager — became the self-appointed surrogate father for his two baby nieces. "He was totally devoted to Kay and her daughters," said his brother, Tony. "Claro spent practically all his time at their house. He was a father without ever having had sex." Claro designated Kay as his next-of-kin when he joined the army so she and his nieces would receive his insurance if he were killed.

Claro graduated from East Moline High School in June 1940, then went to work on the night shift at the John Deere spreader works plant in East Moline. Teachers had encouraged his artistic ambitions, and he did pencil sketches and painted with watercolors in his spare time, even after graduation. After the Japanese attacked Pearl Harbor Claro, twenty, rushed to enlist, telling his oldest brother, Augusto, that he wished he could "earn a star for mother" — which he could only accomplish by getting killed in action. His letters home showed him to be an optimist. "The sun," he wrote from boot camp in Oregon, "never sets if you make it so." Claro was a dedicated, hard-working soldier who rose in just eight months from the rank of buck private to staff sergeant. In another letter home he said he liked his officers, who "treated me like a white person," making him decide that he wanted to become an officer. He wrote home that he "wished there were more like me so that perhaps we could with all the Mexicans in the Army be united and make a regiment."

His letters were, almost to the end, unfailingly upbeat. He described his boot camp as being in "beautiful Oregon" and his next post in "tree-filled Mississippi." When new recruits came to boot camp, Claro wrote: "This is going to be a fighting outfit!" Even when superiors canceled his planned spring furlough and trip home, he said he hoped to "come home when the colors of the rainbow can be seen in the trees." In one of his last letters before being shipped overseas, he wrote that he was concerned that he'd been trained as a supply clerk but would soon be sent into combat without adequate training. Then he wrote: "I got a gun! They gave me a gun — full of grease. Only when we clean the guns do we curse Hitler." When he was shipped overseas, Claro wrote home: "My voyage overseas was as through a sea of calmness. How can a sea be so calm? It is one of the miracles of God — and one of thousands."

Claro belonged to Company E, 120th Infantry Regiment, of the 30th Infantry Division. After arriving in Glasgow, Scotland, on February 22, 1944, the division was deployed along the Scottish coast.

One week after D-Day in June 1944, Claro's unit landed on Omaha Beach, relieving the badly battered 101st Airborne Division and elements of the 29th Infantry Division. His unit was initially ordered to help bury the dead. "Bodies of both Americans and Germans were scattered over the landscape as far as the eye could see," remembered fellow soldier Jack Thacker of the 30th Infantry Division. "We were required to wear gas masks due to the sickening sharp, sweet smell of decaying flesh." Sickening work for "Little Hands" and all involved.

For the next two months, Claro and more than one million Allied soldiers fought through Normandy's *bocage* country, an expanse of small fields bounded by ancient hedgerows. These rows of bushes were exceedingly ancient and had grown thick and tall over the centuries. The Allied High Command knew about them but had underestimated their utility for defense. The Germans didn't make the same mistake and put them to excellent use, turning the region into what quickly became known as "Hedgerow Hell." In the course of battling their way through the hedgerows to the strategic crossroads of St.-Lô, the combat formations of the U.S. First Army (commanded by Gen. Omar Bradley) suffered a total of eleven thousand casualties.

On July 24, 1944, the First Army launched Operation Cobra, a major offensive that would see American forces break free of the bocage country and, subsequently, advance rapidly across northern France to the German frontier. Paving the way for the attack by ground forces was a massive air assault in which heavy bombers of the Eight Air Force were used in a tactical role to carpet-bomb German positions. Medium bombers and fighter-bombers of the Ninth Air Force also took part. In all, more than twenty-three hundred Allied aircraft of all types were involved in the effort, saturating German positions with bombs and rockets in what proved to be (at the time) the most concentrated use of high explosives in U.S. military history. The effects were devastating to the defenders. German historian Paul Carell wrote: "Nothing could withstand [the air attack]." The German Panzer Lehr Division had "at least half its personnel killed, wounded, buried alive or driven out of their minds." Bombs also fell

on American units, killing at least 111 soldiers and wounding another 490. When the bombing stopped, American infantry and
armor went on the attack, advancing through the bomb-ravaged
terrain. The Germans had been ordered to hold their ground, but
their commander, Gen. Fritz Bayerlein recognized that this was
impossible. In his memoirs he wrote: "The long duration of bombing, without any possibility for opposition, created depressions and a
feeling of helplessness, weakness and inferiority. . . . A great number
of men . . . surrendered, deserted to the enemy or escaped to the
rear." Bayerlein declared that the bombing was the worst he had ever
seen: "I don't believe Hell could be as bad."

The Germans retreated rapidly across France with Allied forces
(including Claro's 30th Division) in hot pursuit. In the Battle of the
Falaise Pocket (August 12–21) the Allies captured fifty-thousand
Germans and killed ten thousand. Thousands more were wounded
and the Germans lost most of their heavy equipment, including
tanks. The Allies liberated Paris on August 25. American soldiers
dubbed this swift-moving phase of the war "the rat race." They slept
in muddy foxholes and in elegant châteaus. They ate C and K rations, and they ate "the spoils of war," beef and chicken "liberated"
from French farms; some days they drank water from canteens,
other days they sipped vintage wines "acquired" from the cellars of
French noblemen. On September 2, 1944, Claro's unit was among
the first Allied troops to enter Belgium and, ten days later, to enter
the Netherlands.

The next border was Germany's. Near the German border,
Claro probably saw a sign that read: "Many of you who come up this
road won't be coming back." German artillery fired thousands of
propaganda leaflets into the American lines that read: "What is left
of all this? Nothing! Nothing but days and nights of the heaviest
fighting and for many of you NOTHING BUT A PLAIN WOODEN
CROSS IN FOREIGN SOIL." Claro and the other GIs had to cross
the Siegfried Line, which one American officer described as "undoubtedly the most formidable man-made defense ever contrived.
Its intricate series of dragon's teeth, pillboxes, interconnected communications trenches, gun pits and foxholes . . . provided not only

an excellent defense system but also a base from which to launch a major offensive."

Directly in the path of the Americans' advance, just across the border shared by Belgium, France, and Germany, stood Aachen, Germany's westernmost city. The city held almost no military value, but the Allied High Command believed it would be a major psychological and propaganda victory to capture a large German city. Claro's 30th Division and the 1st Infantry Division were ordered to capture Aachen. In heavy street-to-street fighting, the 30th Division took nine days to advance the last three miles to link up with the 1st Division on October 16, 1944. The Germans finally surrendered on October 21. Though victorious, the battle had exhausted the Americans. The 30th Division had suffered thirty-one hundred casualties, or 20 percent of its strength; and both the 30th and 1st Divisions were judged to be " badly depleted, exhausted, used up" and "in no condition to dash to the Rhine." Claro's unit returned to the rear to rest and prepare for the next round of fighting.

While in the rear, Claro heard talk that Germany would soon surrender, perhaps before Christmas. The British cabinet on September 4, 1944, accepted December 31 as the likely end of the war and military officials in Washington began canceling military contracts, believing the war was all but won. On December 12, 1944, Claro wrote home to his brother: "There is not much to see. Events of the day are dull and burdensome to each of us. Another Christmas is here and for a while I shall think of former days and think of you."

The "dull and burdensome" days ended four days later at 5:30 A.M. when twenty-four divisions of the German Army—including ten panzer divisions—attacked the thinly defended American line in the Ardennes region of eastern Belgium. German forces in the Schnee Eifel sector, located at the geographic center of the offensive, quickly overwhelmed the defenders and raced west, creating the "bulge" in the American lines that gave the battle its name — the Battle of the Bulge. On December 17, the second day of the German offensive, SS troops captured and murdered 140 American soldiers outside the Belgian crossroads town of Malmedy. When President

Franklin D. Roosevelt heard about the massacre, he said: "Now the average GI will hate the Germans just as much as do the Jews." Claro was then forty miles from Malmedy.

During the night of December 17, Claro's unit marched to Malmedy, their route intermittently illuminated by flares dropped by German aircraft. Claro's unit counterattacked to close a twelve-mile gap between Malmedy and St. Vith. At first contact with the Germans, "our outfit broke," said Pvt. John Capano of Claro's 120th Regiment. "When the trouble started, we had no foxholes dug. Suddenly there was the Luftwaffe bombing us. We'd been told the Luftwaffe was washed up. When we heard tanks, we all started to run for cover. We didn't know which way to go. We were firing into the trees. We figured that we just ought to make as much noise as we could." Claro's unit desperately dug foxholes along the Amblève River just west of Malmedy.

December 19, 1944, was "one of the most dismal days of the last year of the war in Europe." Cold temperatures, heavy, low clouds, and news of German advances caused morale to plummet. Nearby Bastogne was surrounded and besieged. As the battle raged, bad weather — snow, fog, and heavy clouds — grounded Allied aircraft. But on the morning of December 23, the Allies got an early Christmas present. A massive high-pressure system cleared the sky of clouds, and Allied air forces resumed operations and wreaked havoc on the enemy.

Claro's unit inched forward. According to company records, "Net advances for the day for these two companies [Claro's E and Company F] were around 300 yards." Nearby Company G made no headway and lost five men, with twenty-four wounded and seven missing. At 3:00 A.M. Christmas Eve, the Germans ran out of fuel and began retreating. When the Americans attacked La Gleize at dawn on Christmas Eve, the enemy had fled — except for a rear guard of about fifty Germans soldiers right in the path of Claro's unit. The official battle report states: "Here some 50 Germans fought fiercely, either because they had not been told that . . . [the Germans] had given up the town, or because they wished to . . . die rather than surrender. They died alright . . . and companies E and G that killed them, had only 10 WIAs [wounded in action] and no KIAs [killed in action]." The Americans captured 172 tanks and 127 prisoners. Snow fell and temperatures dropped to 14 degrees. Claro and his fellow GIs dug foxholes and spent Christmas in them. One American captain, Orval Faubus, wrote home: "This Christmas in embattled Europe will not be remembered long by some, for their memories will die with them."

On December 26, elements of Patton's Third Army broke through the encircling German lines at Bastogne, lifting the siege of that crossroads city. But Hitler refused to allow his troops to withdraw, and during the first eight days of 1945, one of the "greatest artillery battles of the war" was fought near Bastogne. On New Year's Day, Hitler ordered his Luftwaffe into its last great battle of World War II. In the daylight, the skies filled with bombers and fighter planes. German tanks could be heard at almost all hours.

Conditions were cruel to soldiers on both sides. On New Year's Day the temperature plunged to five degrees below zero. It was so cold "we couldn't sleep, so we took our shoes off and took turns sticking our feet under the other guy's armpit," remembered private Jack Pricket. General George Patton prayed to God for better weather, saying, "Sir, this is Patton talking. The last 14 days have been straight hell . . . my soldiers . . . are suffering the tortures of the damned." Journalists dubbed the battle scene the "Valley Forge of World War II."

Heavy snowfalls continued. Waist-high snowdrifts and ice made the narrow roads impassable even for tanks. German and American units fought fierce engagements just to gain possession of buildings in which to sleep — a "battle of billets." When GIs couldn't dig foxholes because the ground was too frozen, they improvised. The army provided two overcoats for every three soldiers. "We placed one overcoat on the ground and three of us lay on it and covered ourselves with the second overcoat," remembered Sgt. John Sweeney. "The only one who was warm was the middle guy so we changed places every twenty minutes or so." Corporal Clair Galdonik remembered that "there were two things in front of you always — the enemy and death. . . . Sometimes morale was so low that you preferred death. . . . When you were wet, cold, hungry, lonely, death looked very inviting."

In mid-January the Red Army resumed offensive operations in Poland. Faced with this renewed threat, the Germans ended offensive operations in the west. But the Germans continued to resist fiercely, and the harsh winter weather continued to make life miserable for everyone. General Leland Hobbs wrote: "We are fighting the weather, and losing about one hundred [men] a day. . . . It's a hell of a country." Lieutenant Joseph Couri remembered January 14 as "the coldest night that I experienced in the war." Claro, like so many soldiers at the time, was emotionally and physically exhausted. On January 18, Claro wrote his brother, "If I come home, I plan to build my home in beautiful Oregon with the angels. If I don't come home, don't forget to donate some money, and say a Mass for me. Be sure to take care of the kids." Claro also urged his brother to tell the men of Little Mexico to join the navy. The brutal realities of war had killed "Little Hand's" romantic idealism.

In his last letter home, dated January 18, 1945, Claro also wrote: "I can see the Germans, but I am not afraid. I can see the eyes of death in front of me, but still I am not afraid." On January 19, 1945, Claro's unit attacked enemy positions in a howling blizzard, driving elements of the 18th Volksgrenadier Division from the crossroads at Recht. Claro was a casualty of that battle. Other than the fact that he was shot and taken to a field hospital, nothing is known of the circumstances in which he fell. The details simply do not exist. A friend rushed to the hospital, but Claro was already dead.

The army buried Claro in plot EEE, row 5, and grave 82 at the United States Military Cemetery in Henri-Chapelle, Belgium. In 1947, the War Department disinterred his body and shipped it home for a funeral on 2nd Street, and burial at the United States Military Cemetery at the Rock Island Arsenal, about five miles from Claro's home.

Claro's will distributed his possessions to his brothers, nieces, and nephews. At death, he owned a ring, a typewriter, and a bicycle. His nieces and nephews rode the bike for years. His sister, Kay, received Claro's military death insurance payment—six months' pay. His parents received the framed gold star Claro had once talked about earning for his mother.

CHAPTER TEN

Boy with the Borrowed, Misspelled Name

Every time it snows . . . I'll think about the Bulge. It brings back memories of the friends I lost and the desperate feelings we had in those days.
— Bart Hagerman, 17th Airborne Division, fifty years after the war

Peter Masias grew up in the shabbiest house on one of the poorest streets in America. His mother and stepfather, perhaps the meanest man on the block, drank away much of the family's money. Peter rarely had shoes that fit or clothes that weren't ragged, and food was far from plentiful. His neighbors, themselves impoverished, took pity and fed and clothed him. Yet, by all accounts, Peter was the nicest, kindest, sweetest-singing boy living on what is now known as Hero Street, U.S.A.

Peter's mother, Epifania "Fanny" Rivas, gave birth to Peter on March 13, 1924, in Lorain, Ohio, an industrial town at the mouth of the Black River on Lake Erie, west of Cleveland. Fanny was born in April 1904 in Mexico, probably in the state of Guanajuato. When she died at age forty-three in February 1948, she was preceded in death by six sons from three marriages. Her first marriage was to a man named Uribe. That marriage produced three children — two sons who apparently didn't survive early childhood and a daughter, Francis, born in 1920. Fanny's second husband was Tomas Rivas, although family members aren't certain about his first name. Fanny and Tomas gave birth to two sons, Peter, and younger brother Raymond, born in 1926. According to family recollections, Tomas Rivas died shortly after Raymond was born, and Fanny then married her third husband, Agapito Masias, who moved the family to Silvis, Illinois, in 1927 to work for the Rock Island Railroad.

Agapito was an illiterate and, by all accounts, a drunkard. The family lived a brief time in a boxcar in the Rock Island Railroad's locomotive repair yard. When the railroad and city officials ordered the boxcar settlement abandoned, the Masias family moved to a tiny house at 124 2nd Street. "It was really just a shack — a couple of rooms with a [wood-burning] stove and dirt floors," said Peter's maternal cousin, Lupe Picon Garcia. She said the boxcar in the rail yard "was probably better housing" than the shack on 2nd Street. Neither the boxcar nor the shack had electricity, running water, or indoor plumbing, but at least the boxcar had a wooden floor and walls that shut out the prairie winds and the winter snows.

Peter was so poor he didn't even own his own name. His stepfather, Agapito Masias, was actually Agapito Macias, but he misspelled the name — or it was misspelled for him — when he first applied for work when he arrived in the United States from Mexico. "We weren't really Masiases, we were Maciases," said Peter's half sister, Mercedes. And Peter was born Peter Rivas, and never had his named legally changed to either Masias or Macias. His friends called him "Peter M." His younger brother joined the navy as Raymond Rivas, but Peter went into the air force during World War II as Peter Masias.

His cousin Lupe Picon Garcia described Peter as "very quiet and shy, but very kind, social and nice." He was "a very, very good person," said his stepsister Mercedes. She described him as "just the nicest person. He was nice when it wasn't easy to be nice. We

Peter Masias

lived in a small, poor home and it wasn't easy. He was kind when there wasn't much kindness around." He is also remembered as the best singer on 2nd Street. "I would take my guitar and climb up to the top of the hill and Peter would come with me," said Louis Ramirez, who lived across the street from Peter on 2nd Street. "We didn't have any money or anyplace to go, so all the boys on the block just spent our time together. I was a pretty good guitar player and Peter was the best singer. He couldn't afford a guitar — he was really poor, worse than the rest of us, who were really poor. We would gather around a fire atop the hill late at night and sing old Mexican songs in Spanish."

Peter's best friend growing up was Luz Segura, who, after his mother died, moved in with his aunt and uncle, Maria and Juan Pompa, up the street from to the Masias home. Luz and Peter did everything together. "We boxed at [Burt] Visconi's boxing club, but we quit after a couple of bouts because we weren't very good. . . . But Visconi hired us to help set up the ring and bring water and towels to the fighters." Once, at bouts at a tavern in Davenport, Iowa, two of the scheduled boxers didn't show up, so Visconi asked Luz and Peter to box each other to fill out the under card. "Peter and I said we were friends and didn't want to fight each other, and Visconi said to just sort of fake it for three rounds and he would pay us, so we did it," Luz recalled. "In the middle of the second round, I hit Peter hard in the face and said 'Whoops — I'm sorry Peter!' and the crowd booed." Peter won the fight, though he hardly laid a glove on Luz, or so says Luz.

Peter and Luz worked odd jobs together, on the railroad and in the onion fields along the Mississippi River in Iowa. After long, hot July days topping onions, the boys would run and dive into the river. One day, Peter dove into shallow water, struck his head on rocks, and had what Luz said was a "five-, six-, maybe eight-inch cut in his head. We had to pull him out of the water. He was kind of groggy. We washed his wound with dirty river water, and that was it. His mother didn't do anything else when he got home — but he lived."

Luz said Peter didn't spend much time at home, because ten people lived in the house. "We could go all up and down the street and the people would share and offer us food. The whole street took care of us," Luz said. Luz said Peter's stepfather was fierce, mean, and angry. Peter's younger half-sister, Mercedes, said, "I remember one time Peter came home from working a job, and he brought his pay home and handed it to our Dad." Usually, kids got some of the money they earned and the family kept the rest. "But our Dad was really, really mean. He just took Peter's money and didn't give him any back. Peter didn't argue, he just went outside and cried."

Peter's cousin, Lupe Picon, and her family lived in Horton, Kansas. One summer, in the middle of the Great Depression, Peter — at about age nine or ten — and his mother, brother Ray, and sister Frances visited the Picon family. "Ray was really unruly, but Peter was very quiet, respectful, and nice." Lupe remembers the first time Peter and his family gathered around the family dinner table. Peter didn't say a word, nor did he touch the food. He just sat perfectly still with his hands folded in his lap.

"My father asked: 'Is anything wrong, Peter?' "

"Peter answered: 'No, sir.' "

"My dad asked: 'Peter, are you feeling all right?' "

"Peter said: 'Yes, sir.' "

"Dad asked: 'Then, why aren't you eating?' "

"Peter said: 'I don't know, sir.' "

"Dad said: 'Peter, go ahead and eat. It's okay.' "

"Peter said: 'Yes, sir.' "

"And he did eat, and he ate well. But only after my dad told him it was okay to eat." Like a young wolf pup around a fresh kill, Peter didn't dare touch the food until the alpha leader growled that it was permissible. "You must understand — our dad was really, really mean," sister Mercedes repeated. "We didn't do anything around him without asking permission. Even then, we were always in trouble."

Peter was not an especially good student, and his illiterate mother and stepfather didn't push him to excel, or even pay any attention to his schooling. Society demanded little of the children of "Little Mexico." Peter's surviving family members don't remember him graduating from high school, and his obituary said only that he "attended Silvis schools." He was seventeen when the United States went to war with Germany, Japan, and Italy. The buildup for the war and the rush of men into the service created a manpower shortage, and Peter got a job at the nearby Rock Island Arsenal, the area's largest employer. He was paid seventy cents an hour, and could work all the overtime he wanted. In March 1942, Peter turned eighteen and the draft board ordered him inducted into the U.S. Army. His half brother, Johnny Masias, told WGN TV in 1972: "He didn't volunteer. He waited to be drafted, but once he was in he was proud to be wearing his airborne wings. He was standing tall. He was proud."

Some of the men signed up for airborne training because they were told honorable service would expunge their criminal records. The airborne program demanded much from trainees. Recruits had to become expert marksmen, parachute packers, and bomb makers. They had to excel in hand-to-hand combat, run five miles in less than fifty minutes, do at least fifty pushups, sixteen chin-ups, and climb a forty-foot rope using only their arms. Paratroopers earned an extra $50 a month in hazard pay — nearly double the pay of an army private.

Peter joined Company C of the 139th Airborne Engineer Battalion, constituted in March 1943 at Camp Mackall, North Carolina, as part of the 17th Airborne Division. Engineers specialized in laying and removing mines, building and destroying bridges — some of the most hazardous duties in World War II. Peter's unit went through intensive paratroop training at the Airborne Jump School at Fort Benning, Georgia. In March 1944, Peter's unit moved to Camp Forest, Tennessee. While many of the paratroopers complained about the boot camp food, Peter enjoyed the first all-you-could-eat menu in his life. Many of the hungry men from 2nd Street said they gained substantial weight during boot camp. And if most of the inductees thought the drill instructors were brutal, Peter didn't; he had trained under a brutal taskmaster all his life, his stepfather.

In August 1944 the 17th Airborne Division was sent to England, where it was placed in strategic reserve. Some of the paratroopers feared they'd missed the war — that all the fighting had ended, or would soon. Then, in the predawn hours of December 16, 1944, the Germans launched their Ardennes offensive. Shortly thereafter the paratroopers were rousted from their beds to begin "feverish preparations" for movement to the Continent. But bad weather intervened, grounding the division's aircraft for a week. Finally, on Christmas Eve, 1944, the 17th Airborne Division — known as "Thunder from Heaven" — flew at night from England to Reims, France. On Christmas Day 1944, Peter and his fellow paratroopers rushed via truck — rather than by air, glider, or parachute — to defensive positions in France along the Meuse River from Givet to Verdun. Their division was assigned to Gen. George Patton's Third Army, racing to break the German encirclement of Bastogne. Bitterly cold temperatures greeted the paratroopers, and the winter moon cast eerie shadows on snow-covered fields. But the skies were clear, allowing American air power to strike hard at the enemy. December 24 saw "the greatest concentrated confrontation of air forces during the entire European War." In many places in the Ardennes heavy fighting continued through the night. One GI wrote home: "The shells and flares light up the sky and the tracers cut thousands of gleaming paths across the Christmas heavens. When the hubbub subsides the pale, cold Christmas moon is still shining," adding, "the Christmas fireworks were unlike any we had seen before or since."

Heavy snow fell on the 28th, and for four days aircraft on both sides were grounded. But fighting in the snow-covered fields and forests of Ardennes raged on. On January 1, 1945, Hitler said on German radio: "Our people are resolved to fight the war to victory under any and all circumstances. . . . The world must know that this state will. . . never capitulate." That same day, Peter's unit assembled in below-zero temperatures near Neufchâteau, Luxembourg, about nineteen miles southwest of Bastogne. On January 3 Peter's unit marched through heavy snow to an area just west of Bastogne. The night was clear and cold, the moon "unimaginably bright." The wind-chill plunged to sixty degrees below zero and some forty-six thousand American soldiers suffered cases of trench foot. A 17th Airborne paratrooper, Brice Jordan, wrote his wife: "I wonder sometimes how I kept from freezing. It was a job trying to keep warm. I always dreaded to see night come because we couldn't have a fire."

The 17th Airborne Division saw its first combat on the morning of Thursday, January 4, 1945. Patton ordered the division to strike north toward Flamizoulle and the Ourthe River, with the 194th Glider Infantry attacking on the left, the 513th Regiment attacking on the right — and Peter's 139th Airborne Engineer Battalion out in front of both units, clearing the mine fields. The engineers had their work cut out for them — the Germans had seeded the area liberally with the deadly devices. General William "Bud" Miley, the division commander, said that the Germans "put more mines and booby traps over this area than I had ever thought possible and we lost a lot of men to them. There are . . . mines under every tree. We haven't been able to move without an engineer sweep in front of us." The man responsible for mining the area was German General-almajor Otto-Ernst Remer, commander of the elite Panzer Führer-Begleitbrigade. "For my money," said Miley, Remer was "the prize son-of-a-bitch in this war."

Just before the 17th Division started its attack, Patton told Miley: "There's nothing out in front of you." Miley privately responded: "Then who cut to pieces the 11th Armored and the 87th Infantry Divisions when they were attacked over this same terrain a few hours earlier?" Patton also told Miley the German opposition would be made up of very old or very young men; instead, the paratroopers would be going up against Remer's battle-hardened Waffen SS troops.

It was cold and a light snow was falling when the 17th Division's supporting artillery began softening up the piney woods three hundred yards in front of Peter's unit. Peter and his fellow paratroopers moved out at 8:15 A.M., crawling slowly forward through the snow and ice toward the enemy positions in the woods. German troops attacked unexpectedly from the woods, and mayhem ensued. The paratroopers wore dark brown coats that stood out against the snow, making them perfect targets for German machine gunners and riflemen. Paratrooper Bart Hagerman recalled: "People didn't crumble and fall like they did in Hollywood movies. They were tossed in the air. They were whipped around. They were hit to the ground hard and their blood splattered everywhere. And a lot of people were standing close to people and found themselves covered in the blood and flesh of their friends."

The attacking battalions lost 40 percent of their strength in their first day of battle.

On January 6, the 17th Airborne went on the defensive, with Peter's unit positioned on the division's left flank. But Patton insisted that German resistance was light, and ordered another attack. Just after daybreak on January 7, "the aggressive but green paratroopers" rushed Rechrival and Flamierge. Withering enemy fire killed over one hundred men. By dusk they had taken Flamierge. That night, starting at 10:00 P.M., the Germans pounded them with artillery. On January 8, the Germans counterattacked with infantry supported by some twenty tanks, driving the Americans out of the town and into the woods. "We had people running everywhere, jumping and running . . . and holding their hands up and giving up," remembered paratrooper Willis Grice. Survivors hid in the open fields, lying in knee-deep snow for up to forty-eight hours without food or sleep. Incredibly, Patton asserted that the Germans were retreating. To which Miley responded: "It doesn't look like the enemy is withdrawing."

The 17th Airborne went on the defensive once again. On January 9 two feet of snow fell and the temperature dropped to six degrees below zero. Many suffered frozen feet. Bart Hagerman of remembered: "Their feet were just as black as coal . . . maybe gunsteel blue if you want to put it that way. And in the first stages, they swell quite a bit, but after that, when they start turning blue and everything, they get almost flat. It kind of turns your stomach." The Germans, Patton told his staff, "are colder, hungrier and weaker than we, to be sure. But they are still doing a great piece of fighting."

Patton struck with eight divisions, advancing northward from Bastogne. The 17th Airborne captured Mande St. Etienne and

Flamizoulle. Casualties were heavy, but the Germans began to cave. Finally, on January 11, German troops began withdrawing from the Bastogne area, leaving behind eighty-four minefields for Peter and the other American engineers to clear. The Germans' favorite mines were motion-sensitive butterfly bombs that were so sensitive that just blowing on them could set them off. One engineer, J. D. Jones, described the defusing procedure: "I worked with cleaning up mine-fields. That would make you sweat a little bit down the back, I tell you. We'd find a handle [on the mine], and then put up a stick, run a piece of rope with a bent nail and put that hook up around the handle, get off a ways, and pull it. And of course it would blow."

Most German forces in the 17th Airborne's area of operations withdrew on January 12. However, a sizeable contingent remained in the vicinity of Flamierge. On January 12, Patton once again ordered the 17th Airborne to take Flamierge. At 8:30 A.M. January 13, in bitter cold and fog, the 17th Airborne began its third and final attack to clear the Germans from what was called "Dead Man's Ridge." By 10:45 A.M., Flamierge was again in American hands. But the victory was costly, with the 17th Airborne losing 1,117 enlisted men and 63 officers — 54 percent of the division's strength — since arriving in the battle zone just after New Year's Day.

Despite its losses the 17th stayed in the fight. From January 18 to February 10, the division attacked enemy units in Houffalize, Watteremal, Espeler, and in the Luxembourg towns of Eschweiler and Cleraux; it also cleared the Germans from the west bank of the Our River. Peter helped remove roadblocks, defuse mines, build bridges, and drive bulldozers through snow drifts.

British Prime Minister Winston Churchill told the House of Commons on January 18 that the Battle of the Bulge was "undoubt-edly the greatest American battle of the war and will, I believe, be regarded as an ever-famous American victory." Some six hundred thousand men from twenty-nine infantry divisions and six armored divisions took part in the battle. Not without cost. "The 17th Airborne was . . . mauled in heavy fighting around Bastogne during the terrible fight there in early January. The airborne divisions were so badly mauled that they were not available as paratroop forces for

two months." Fifty years later, 17th Airborne veteran Bart Hagerman recalled, "Every time it snows . . . I'll think about the Bulge. It
brings back memories of the friends I lost and the desperate feelings we had in those days."

Peter survived. The 17th Division was relieved of frontline duty and,
on Sunday, February 11, 1945, after a night of steady rain, the
paratroopers — most suffering from exposure, fatigue, and
malnutrition — climbed into trucks and rode to Alron, Belgium.
Then they moved to a tent city at a French airfield near Chalons-sur-
Marne, where the men ate their first hot meals in eight weeks and
bathed for the first time in weeks — "and nobody wanted to get out of
the water either," said one veteran. Replacements arrived, and some
wounded veterans returned to duty — evidence that Peter's unit
wasn't going home. The men ate well, tracked down buddies, and
practiced parachuting out of airplanes. But the war and the dying
weren't over.

Peter turned twenty-one years old on March 13, 1945. That
same day rumors swept the tent city that the 17th Airborne was
going to finally make its first combat jump. Then came orders for
"Operation Varsity" — Field Marshal Montgomery's plan to drop
17,122 American and British paratroopers on the southern edge of
the Diesfordter Forest just across the Rhine River. The airborne
force was to secure the high ground on the east bank of the Rhine
River and capture six bridges over the nearby River Issel. Meantime,
sixty thousand troops would assault across the Rhine and link up
with paratroopers.

The Germans somehow learned about the forthcoming operation and on March 23 "Axis Sally," broadcasting from Berlin,
taunted the Americans: "Hi, all you good-looking guys in the 17th
Airborne Division in France. The British are getting you ready to be
slaughtered for the greater glory of their King and Empire, aren't
they? . . . We know you're coming tomorrow and we know where
you're coming — at Wesel. Ten crack divisions from the Russian
front will be a reception committee to greet you." The propaganda
war was backed up by live ammo. Behind the Rhine's banks and

beyond the reach of Allied artillery, 367 German antiaircraft units readied some one thousand guns for action against the Allied air armada.

March 24, 1945, was clear and cold; at daybreak, the tempera-ture was near freezing. Winds blew twenty to twenty-five miles per hour — unfavorable conditions for flying and parachuting. Officers roused the weary paratroopers well before dawn and fed the men big steaks and apple pie — sure signs that a major battle loomed. Peter pulled a green M-43 combat suit over a brown wool shirt and trou-sers, and strapped a trench knife to one leg. Wearing a standard steel helmet, Peter stuffed British Gammon grenades, three days worth of K rations, and two days worth of D rations into his deep pockets. Peter likely carried a M-1 rifle, plenty of ammunition, and a shovel. Perhaps, rather than a rifle, his platoon leader ordered Peter to carry a bazooka or machine gun. Then the paratroopers waited. Shortly after 6:00 A.M., Peter boarded a truck and rode to the planes. At one of the hangars, he drew a parachute, probably a T-7, which most of the paratroopers had used in practice jumps. Then, more waiting. The first American paratrooper unit left at 7:17 A.M., roar-ing off in C-47s, twin-engine transport planes nicknamed "Gooney Birds." The airborne artillery units followed, then the combat engi-neers, including Peter's 139th Airborne Engineer Battalion. The master plan called for Peter and the rest of the 139th AEB to para-chute north of Wesel in Landing Zone S, a large flat area where the Issel River and the Issel Canal merge, then capture the bridge over the Issel and protect the division's right flank.

The 17th Airborne "Thunder from Heaven" armada left from seventeen airfields around Paris. The British Red Devils left from eleven airfields in England. The combined armada included 1,572 transport planes and 1,326 gliders — all escorted by 889 fighter planes. En route, some of the planes picked up another broadcast by Axis Sally: "Men of the 17th Airborne Division, we know you are coming. We are waiting and ready for you on the Rhine. You won't need a parachute. The flak will be so thick you can walk down." The 17th Airborne air column alone took almost two hours and twenty minutes to pass overhead and consisted of 226 C-47s and 72 C-46s carrying paratroopers, plus 906 gliders towed by 610 C47s. British Prime Minister Winston Churchill and Supreme Allied Commander Gen. Dwight Eisenhower were on the ground to watch the armada fly overhead. Also on the ground was Peter's childhood friend, Luz Segura, who was with the U.S. 2nd Armored Division. "We cheered wildly as the planes flew overhead. We knew we were finally crossing the Rhine. I didn't know that Peter was in one of those planes," Segura told the author sixty years later.

As the Allied armada crossed the Rhine at less than one thousand feet, intense ground fire blasted Allied aircraft, and descending paratroopers and gliders. Despite clear skies, pilots couldn't identify the jump areas, which were obscured by smoke from the German antiaircraft guns. Also, Allied shelling and bombing the day before had knocked down many landmarks the pilots were supposed to use. Worse still, the new C-46s didn't have self-sealing fuel tanks. Hit by antiaircraft fire, they tended to burst into flames. The C-46s, nicknamed "flying coffins," became "flaming coffins."

Some of the lead aircraft overflew their jump areas. Many were struck by enemy ack-ack. Following aircraft had to pull up or away from the lead airplanes. At four hundred feet paratroopers finally jumped into fierce enemy fire. "We were raked with heavy machine-gun fire while we were descending in our chutes," one paratrooper remembered. Trees and power lines snared parachutes. Even when they landed on flat ground, paratroopers were easy targets during the time it took to unfasten leg straps and harnesses. Some paratroopers were "streamers" — their chutes never opened. Some died when their planes crashed before the drop zone. Others died in ground combat when they faced German artillery, infantry and tanks. Paratroopers who avoided the ack-ack and machine-gun fire engaged in "countless small, vicious firefights" on the ground. Someplace in this chaos, twenty-one-year-old Pfc. Peter Masias of Silvis, Illinois, died. The 17th Airborne suffered 834 men wounded, 282 men missing and 393 men killed during the day. Peter is listed in the 139th Airborne Engineer Battalion's Roll of Honor.

Historians questioned the need for Operation Varsity. "[T]he critical need of the operation had been overcome before the troops became airborne," wrote Major Robert Corey, assistant G-2 of the 17th Airborne Division. Corey believed the British land forces, which had crossed the Rhine River twelve hours before the paratroopers dropped "had been so successful that there was no doubt of the success of the Rhine crossing before the (17th Division) started." The British Ninth Army had crossed the Rhine with relatively light casualties. Historian Kirk B. Ross wrote: "Operation Varsity may be seen as simply a lavish attempt by British airborne planners to redeem themselves for their failure to secure a bridgehead over the Rhine at Arnhem the previous September at Operation Market-Garden. Though successful within its limited scope, the contributions . . . rendered by Varsity, in the end, had not been worth the cost."

Peter's younger half-sister, Lupe, believes that Peter's spirit returned home after he died. "One night, right after we learned that Peter had been killed, I was awakened by a shimmering pale light in the room where Peter had slept. I could see someone sitting in the pale light, taking off his big boots and laying down to sleep in Peter's bed," Lupe said. "And I knew that Peter had come home." He was buried, temporarily, in an Allied military cemetery near Wesel. In 1949, the Army disinterred Peter's body and ship it to Silvis, then buried him with full military honors at the U.S. Military Cemetery at the Rock Island Arsenal in August 1949. His body lies there today, under his borrowed, misspelled name.

CHAPTER ELEVEN

The Last Battle

From the crossing of the Rhine to the end of the war, every man who died, died needlessly.
— Historian Stephen E. Ambrose

In their wheel-less red boxcar, with the help of Mexican midwives, Angelina Sandoval gave birth to her first American-born child, Joseph, on a cold prairie night on March 8, 1919. It had been eighteen months since she and Eduviges moved into the Silvis rail yard, and Joseph's birth softened the pain of homesickness and the loss of their first two children in Mexico. They were starting over. Eduviges had a good-paying job, they had a roof over their heads — albeit it was the roof of a discarded boxcar — and now Angelina had birthed a son. Joseph was the beginning of a large, devoted family.

Eduviges nicknamed Joseph *Estrellito* — Little Star — because, in his eyes, Joe shined so brightly. Joe learned to speak at an early age, first in Spanish and then, after he started school, he quickly learned to read and write the Anglos' language. Hardly anyone in Little Mexico spoke, read, and wrote in English. So as early as six or seven, Joseph started handling the Sandoval family's financial, legal, and tax matters. "My dad depended on him to do everything," said

Tanilo, Joseph's younger brother by seven years. "Joe opened and read the mail. He paid the taxes, and went with my dad if there was anything to do with the government. Dad trusted Joe with everything." Neighbors in the rail yard borrowed Joe to help them translate English-language documents. Little Joseph had the status as almost an adult within the family, and within Little Mexico.

Eduviges gave Joe great responsibility. Tanilo remembers his first great adventure outside Little Mexico — going with Joe across the Mississippi River to purchase winter coats for the family on a Saturday, late in the autumn of either 1931 or 1932. Tanilo was just five or six years old, Joe just twelve or thirteen. The Great Depression was at its depths, and money was desperately scarce. But the children needed coats before winter came. Eduviges, who earned thirty-five cents an hour working for the financially troubled Rock Island Railroad, handed young Joseph a couple of dollars — a fortune at the time — and told him to be "mas cuidoso, mas prudente" — very careful, very prudent. Then the brothers left their house at 187 2nd Street, walked down to 1st Avenue and waited for the electric-powered streetcar.

Eduviges watched as Joe held Tanilo's hand and the two brothers boarded the electric streetcar that carried them away. The streetcar took them along what was then U.S. Highway 6 some twelve miles through East Moline and Moline into the county seat of Rock Island. Joseph and Tanilo then jumped off the streetcar and walked a short distance to the Illinois side of the Government Bridge, a two-tiered steel drawbridge which crosses over the western edge of Arsenal Island and then spans the Mississippi River more than fifteen hundred feet into downtown Davenport, Iowa. Davenport's then-population of over sixty thousand residents made it the largest city between Chicago and Des Moines. The little boys dodged automobiles and walked past bread lines as they found their way to a red-stone, five-story department store at the intersection of Main and 2nd Street. They carefully examined the sale items, figured the costs, and debated who could wear what coats. Then Joe bought coats that would be in the family for years to come. Toting their purchases, Joe and Tanilo backtracked their route and returned home — after

Joseph Sandoval

about five hours — to hugs and tears from Angelina, and even Eduviges. "Joe took me on my first great adventure. He was always my hero," said Tanilo.

As he grew older, Joseph didn't like the way his family lived. The house the family moved into in 1929 had a dirt main floor, no plumbing or running water, and no electricity. Initially, the two-story house on 2nd Street was little different in creature comforts than Eduviges' hut on the hacienda, or the family boxcar in the rail yard. Angelina and her daughters carried water from spigots across the street to scrub the huge family's laundry by hand. Angelina cooked meals in the walk-out basement over a potbellied wood-burning stove that also heated the house. An outhouse on the hill behind their home served as toilets. Chicken and lambs wandered the hillside yard and neighborhood, penned in only at night. "Dad didn't mind living like that," Tanilo said. "Coming from Mexico and from the yard, he didn't know any different. Neither did mom."

But Joe saw more in America, and he wanted to live like an American. As soon as he could, Joe started working part-time jobs, as a "gandy dancer," helping lay and repair railroad tracks, or picking onions in the summer heat in the fields across the Mississippi River, or working as a janitor. He and his brother, Frank, pooled their savings and started fixing up the house. Joe and Frank paid an electrician to bring power into the house. They improved the flooring in the basement. Then the brothers brought running water into the house. Joe also wanted to end the near-daily scene of his mother and sisters sitting on the front steps washing the family clothes without running water. "Joe always worried [that] my mom worked too hard, so he bought her a washing machine," Tanilo said. "Then he bought her a Philco radio with push buttons. She couldn't understand the words, but she liked the music. She wouldn't let us play it on Sundays, or any time after the boys went to war. All you could hear after the boys went to war was mom crying."

Joseph's younger sister, Georgia, remembers him as being "tall with curly hair. On his way home from work [at the International Harvester plant], he would drop by the house and leave mom a piece of fruit, probably something he saved from his lunch. On paydays, he'd come by our house and hide some money for my mom. He'd maybe put a silver dollar on a rafter or a railing along the stairs. Then he'd come back and ask her if she'd found what he'd left. If she hadn't, he'd go show her." Tanilo added: "Mom always worried about Joe, too. She always tried to give him extra food for his lunch. And later, when he first got inducted [into the Army in 1944], there was some problem with his pay, he wasn't getting paid right. So Mom sent him a dollar, and he sent it back to her and wrote that he was fine and he didn't need her money, and not to worry. They were very close."

Another woman came into Joe's life. Against his mother's strong wishes, Joe married Nellie in 1942. Joe built a tiny addition onto the back of his parents' house on 2nd Street — a bedroom, small kitchen, and a bathroom. "Mom never liked Nellie, but then Mom never liked any of the girls the boys brought home or any of the boys the girls brought home," Tanilo said. "I'm sure it was hard on Nellie living in the same house with mom. If mom had her way, none of us ever would have got married. And Joe, he was her favorite."

In 1943, Joe and Nellie had a son, Henry. In the spring of 1944 Nellie got pregnant again — with a son, Mike. Initially, being the head of a household and a father earned Joe a draft deferment. But in the spring of 1944, with the Allies planning the invasion of Europe, the military needed more men, and draft deferments were lifted. The U.S. Army drafted Joe, and on May 13, 1944, he was posted to Fort McClellan, Alabama. He got a two-week furlough in June, which he used to come home for the last time.

In July, his unit was shipped to Britain as replacements in the 1st Battalion of the 41st Armored Infantry Regiment, part of the 2nd Armored Division. The army quickly assigned Joe's unit to France, to help fight the second stage of the invasion of Normandy. The army had trained Joe as a rifleman to accompany Sherman tanks into battle in the hedgerows near Normandy. The 41st Infantry reported that it was difficult to motivate infantrymen — many of them green soldiers like Joe — to follow the tanks into the hedgerows. General

Omar Bradley said of the hedgerows: "Isn't this the damnedest country you ever saw? . . . It's as bad as some of the stuff on Guadal[canal]. Heavy underbrush with thick hedges. Germans in position under the hedges and it is necessary to root him out when he persists in sticking, as he frequently does." On August 5, Joe wrote home from France and told his family not to worry as the Allied armies had broken out from the hedgerow country in Normandy. Operation Cobra had forced the Germans to retreat from Normandy.

But on August 6, 1944, the Germans surprised the Allies, attacking with seven crack panzer units in hopes of splitting the American First and Third Armies. The surprise counterattack near Mortain, France, left the 2nd Battalion of the 120th Infantry—the "Lost Battalion"—isolated for almost three weeks. The Allies rushed troops and tanks—including Joe's unit—to free the Lost Battalion. Conditions were hot and dry during the day, but cold and damp in the early morning hours: "A bad time indeed to be lying wounded in the damp, open fields of Normandy as some certainly are," wrote Lt. Orval Faubus. On August 9, 1944, Joe's unit helped capture a strategic hill east of Mortain. Then, at 6:50 P.M. on August 10, eight German tanks accompanied by infantrymen rumbled down the road where the bulk of Joe's unit had dug in. In a fierce tank battle, five of the German tanks were destroyed, and the other three withdrew. Infantry from the 21st SS Panzergrenadier Regiment infiltrated the defenses at night and tossed grenades at the American's foxholes. On August 11, the 41st Armored Infantry—Joe's unit—moved forward, but encountered heavy German fire just several hundred yards from the American lines. Joe's unit was surrounded and pinned down by German machine-gun fire. The Americans struck back with tank and artillery fire that allowed Joe and his fellow GIs to race back to the American lines. On Sunday, August 13, the Germans pulled out. To cover the retreat, German tanks blasted away at Joe's entrenched unit. That night, the German rear guard troops slipped behind American lines and fired point-blank into foxholes. At daylight, with the support of American bombers and fighter-bombers, the Americans took to the offense. Joe and the other infantrymen followed Sherman tanks against two regiments of German tanks and infantry. Allied planes dropped bombs, and American artillery pounded the enemy. The Americans beat back repeated German counterattacks until, at about 6:30 P.M., the Germans withdrew. Joe's regiment would be awarded a Presidential Citation for valor for its actions that day.

After the Germans pulled out, Joe and his unit went behind the front lines to recuperate. He wrote home on August 18, 1944, in English and Spanish asking about his baby sons, his wife, and his mother and father. On August 24 Joe wrote his younger brother Frank — his first best friend, his playmate in the red boxcar and in the Silvis rail yard — a letter. "Dear Frank . . . take care of yourself." But it was too late. Frank had been machine-gunned to death in June 1944 in Burma. However, the Sandoval family wasn't notified of his death until late August. Joe learned of Frank's death on September 11. On September 14 he wrote a sister: "I bet he [dad] is really taking it hard about Frank. And Mother, I bet she's been even sick after hearing about Frank. . . . I couldn't believe it. I read it over and over, and I'm telling you I started to cry. . . . You kids ought to try and make Ma forget so it ain't so hard on her. Tell the boys to help her and my Dad at least until I get home, and I hope with God's help I'll be home soon. . . . Tell the girls not to forget to pray for me." On September 20, Joe wrote home: "Tell my Ma I'm OK and not to worry. Well you know people here wear wooden shoes we read about. I don't know how they can wear them." On September 24, Joe wrote and said: "Don't feed Henry [his baby son] too much. Don't let him get sick."

Joe's regiment then sped across France to the German border. It would receive a second presidential citation for its role in breaking Germany's Siegfried Line east of the Roer River. The fighting along the Siegfried Line was intense. The regimental commander, Lt. Col. Etter, and executive officer, Maj. Berra, were killed by shell fire. Joe received his first purple heart when he was wounded — his family never learned the gravity of the wound or how it was inflicted. Joe wrote home from an unidentified English hospital on November 30, telling his father, in Spanish, not to worry. He wrote a sister on December 9 that he'd been "hit in the leg. Tell my Mom and Dad that it's nothing." Joe spent Christmas 1944 in the English hospital. Ordinarily, Joe's wound might have earned him a discharge. But the Battle of the Bulge was then raging, and American forces in the Ardennes were suffering enormous losses. So doctors treated the wounded and returned those who had healed to the front.

On February 22, 1945, he wrote home: "I am starting to move again . . . leaving this place tomorrow morning." On February 27, he wrote: "They're moving me." On March 6, he wrote home from "somewhere in France." He was being sent back to his unit, back to the front. Joe spent his twenty-sixth birthday, March 8, 1945, in the ruins of Germany. On March 17, in his last known letter, Joe wrote home: "Moving now." He complained of receiving no mail and asked: "Has [sic] Hank and Mike been over to see you?"

Joe witnessed vast carnage. Allied aircraft had dropped millions of tons of bombs on major German cities. Millions of young German soldiers had been killed in combat. The war had cost Joe much, too. By April 1945, he knew of the deaths of his brother Frank in Burma, and his neighborhood friends Tony Pompa in Italy, and Willie Sandoval along the Belgian-German border. He likely didn't know about his friend Claro Solis' death in January in the Battle of the Bulge, or Peter Masias' death just days earlier in Germany. New friends and comrades in his unit also had been killed, and he saw wounded men die at the military hospital in Britain.

The end of the war was approaching. More than three hundred thousand German soldiers surrendered in mid-April in the Ruhr pocket. Elsewhere, though, many German units "fought fiercely and inflicted great damage."

On the morning of April 11, 1945, Joe's regiment left Liebenberg, Germany, and barreled sixty miles to the west bank of Elbe River near the town of Schoenbeck. One GI recounted the scene: "The spring is here in its fullness, the fruit trees and flowers in bloom and, after last night's heavy showers, the pale green foliage [is] shining it all its new spring freshness. . . . All along the roads are the refugees, the slave laborers, now freed by our advancing armies." Joe's unit halted upon reaching the Elbe. The Allies had agreed to the partition of postwar Germany, with everything east of the Elbe going to the Soviets, so Eisenhower ordered advancing American forces to halt on the river's west bank. The Allied High Command had also agreed that the Russian Army would capture Berlin, and that the American Army would advance no further. Joe and his fellow soldiers were told the war was effectively over! A joyous celebration broke loose. The officers and men hugged each other. They cheered and fired guns in the air. Some even cried for joy. The celebration was raucous, especially after a cache of wine and liquor was found. The war was over, and they were alive.

But the war wasn't over.

The next day, the 41st Infantry Regiment received orders to return to duty. The Germans had destroyed all bridges over the Elbe, and the regimental command wanted to build a bridge that would span the river. Mike Ariano, of the 41st Infantry Regiment, recounted: "Many of the GIs who were out celebrating what was thought to be the end of the war for us were not aware of the alert and we had to search the town for them." Confusion reigned. Not only was the war not over, unit communications broke down. Artillery fire couldn't be coordinated because the battalion's radio died. "From the perspective of the infantryman involved," Ariano wrote, "the Elbe river crossing was an operation that started in confusion and ended in confusion." Lieutenant Colonel Carlton E. Stewart wrote: "We had absolutely no idea what our mission was to be. I received the shortest order I have ever received in my life. It was simple, 'Cross the river and be in reserve in the little patch of woods, just across the other side of the river.' I had no communications with the parent outfit, no armor, and no clear idea of what was required of me."

Joe and other infantrymen loaded into nine rubber assault boats at 9:30 P.M. on April 12 and crossed over to the east bank without incident, completing the operation in about an hour. Then, engineers started building a bridge needed so American tanks could cross the river. At first, the Americans met no resistance, but after daybreak, German artillery zeroed in on the partially built bridge.

Five bridge floats were destroyed by German artillery. On the eastern shore of the Elbe, the American soldiers met "meager resistance" at first, then ran into "heavy fire ... forcing them to drop back and build up a line behind the levee." Allied artillery helped force the Germans to retreat. The GIs then spotted some forty German soldiers advancing to the battle zone. Joe's unit held their fire until the Germans were very close, "at which time every available weapon opened up for a matter of seconds. A few of the Germans were killed while the remainder gave up without a single loss" to Joe's unit. Joe's unit had no way to get the German POWs back behind American lines as German artillery continued to stymie the U.S. engineer's efforts to complete the bridge.

German shell fire became so intense that at 2:00 P.M. on April 13, the attempt to build the bridge was ordered abandoned. The American riflemen — including Joe — were stranded on the east bank without tanks, artillery, air support, boats, or a bridge back to their own lines. Then, five German tanks accompanied by infantrymen arrived on the scene, heading straight for Joe's unit. "The tanks took cover ... and started shooting direct fire" into Joe's unit. Other German tanks circled and flanked the Americans and began firing at the riflemen. American commanders ordered their men to retreat, and Joe's unit moved south toward Grunewald and Elbenau, which had been set on fire by shell fire from both sides. Regimental headquarters then ordered the Americans to establish another bridgehead to the south near Grunewalde. Lieutenant Colonel John W. Finnel, commanding officer, 1st Battalion, 41st Armored Infantry Regiment (and task force commander), said: "My one question was whether it would be that night and they said 'Yes.' I also may have added, 'Are you kidding?' " The order was issued at 11:00 P.M., April 13. Ariano wrote that "we all were exhausted and some men [were] so bad off that when we stopped for a break it took pleading to get them moving again."

German tanks, troops and artillery drove U.S. combat engineers away from the second proposed bridge site on April 14. Major James R. McCartney of the 17th Armored Engineers Battalion reported that the German defense was "determined and heavy. . . . The enemy . . . launched a well-coordinated attack." Joe and the American infantrymen were isolated with no air or tank support. Just as dawn broke, German tanks and infantry attacked. The tanks stopped just outside of bazooka range and opened fire on the GIs. Joe and his fellow soldiers hid in cellars as the tanks blasted away. By 11:30 A.M., "the [41st] Armored Infantry, fighting without antitank weapons, other than bazookas, disintegrated into isolated groups and were no longer an effective fighting force," said the official army report. Joe and the other GIs fled toward the swift-running, 450-foot-wide river. Ariano wrote: "Once we got to the river the question was how to get across, the current looked awful and swift. . . . We were at an unused boat dock and having no apparent options we decided to swim across. We took off our combat trousers, boots and cartridge belts and dropped our rifles into the river and started [swim]. I was an excellent swimmer but I didn't realize how weakened I was from exhaustion and lack of sleep and food. I had to fight the desire to just give up and drown. . . . This operation was the end of combat for our battalion. It was pretty well chopped up. Our company alone had about 60 MIAs."

The official army report said the 2nd Armored Division lost six killed, 23 wounded, and 147 missing. Joe Sandoval was initially one of the missing. One year later, the army recovered and identified Joe's body and declared him killed in action. The army awarded him his second purple heart and a bronze star, but couldn't tell Joe's family how he had died — whether he had been shot, killed by shellfire, or drowned. They didn't know Joe had celebrated war's end just hours before he died.

Joseph Sandoval, the Little Star of Little Mexico, and U.S. President Franklin Roosevelt, the leader of the free world, died within hours of each other. Two weeks later, on April 30, 1945, Adolph Hitler committed suicide in his bunker in Berlin. On May 2, the Red Army captured Berlin. On May 7, Germany surrendered. President Truman declared May 8 to be Victory Day in Europe. But there was no celebration at 187 2nd Street in Silvis, Illinois. Frank wasn't coming home, and, now, neither was his brother, Joseph.

Before he went overseas, Joe had given his mother a Philco radio. The family used it to follow war news and listen to music. After Joe died, his mother forbade the family from turning the radio on. No Joe, no music, no joy at 187 2nd Street. "It was very sad for me when they told me my son was going to leave for war," Angelina told a reporter many years later. "And I still feel sad about it."

CHAPTER TWELVE

Bunker Hill, Korea

The Chinese have come in with both feet.
— President Harry Truman

As war raged across Europe, Asia and, the Pacific, enemy troops back home held Billy Goat Hill. They had been driven off time and again. But now the enemy troops were back, and it was Joe Gomez's duty — once again — to lead the charge to drive them off the hill. Joe's unit gathered between Honey Creek and Billy Goat Hill — so-called because some claimed it too steep to climb except by goats. Joe was the toughest of the attackers, and he organized and led the charge. He loved it. Between battles, all he talked about was going to war and taking hills from the enemy. "Charge!" he yelled, and his troops swarmed up Billy Goat Hill. Ammunition fired from all angles. "Ow — I'm hit!" "Ouch, I'm down!" Cries came from the attackers and the defenders. The little crab apples the boys threw at each other hurt!

The boys of Little Mexico used Billy Goat Hill between 2nd and 3rd Streets for many things. Before they enlisted or were drafted, older boys dug caves in the hill that they used as hideaways. They built fires at the peak of the hill, drank smuggled beer, and sang

119

songs late into the night. In the daytime — especially after December 7, 1941 — younger boys of Little Mexico used the hill to play war. They fought the 3rd Street boys, who, by all accounts, were smaller, weaker, and not as tough as the 2nd Street boys. To make up the difference the 3rd Street boys started at the top of the hill, while the 2nd Street boys charged from the bottom with orders to "take the hill." Both sides fought with tiny inedible crab apples that were readily available. Almost always, the 2nd Street boys took the hill, and the toughest of their warriors, the fiercest of the hill takers, was Joe Gomez.

Joe's parents, Ambrosia and Amanda Gomez, fled devastated Leon, Mexico, during the revolution and lived in a settlement of boxcars in the Silvis rail yard where they raised ten children, seven boys and three girls. Their third child, Joe, was born on an historic date — November 13, 1929 — the day the New York Stock Exchange prices hit the low for the year, triggering the Great Depression. Joe — conceived in the family's boxcar home but born in a little house on 2nd Street — was a big boy. Ultimately, Joe would stand five feet ten inches — perhaps the tallest boy on the block. "School was something he had to do, but didn't really like," said his younger brother Raul "Buddy" Gomez. "He had lots of friends, and lots of girlfriends. He was mostly quiet, but he was aggressive when he got mad. He had a temper . . . but he wasn't a bully. If he was your friend, nobody messed with you." Joe and Raul took boxing lessons, and won most of their fights. "Nobody wanted to fight Joe," Raul said. "He was a natural born fighter who could take a punch."

Death surrounded Joe's home at 181 2nd Street. Six boys on the street died in World War II, including Tony Pompa — who lived directly across the street — and Frank and Joseph Sandoval — who lived two doors up the street. Joe also knew the other three boys on the block who died in World War II — Claro Solis, Willie Sandoval, and Peter Masias. While the old people in the little houses that dotted the street grieved, the young boys still hungered for war as American soldiers. Joe's parents promised him he could join the

Joseph Gomez

military after he turned seventeen. "He was very patriotic — we all were. We wanted to serve our country," said his brother. "All the boys dreamed of going into combat." Joe enlisted into the U.S. Army on November 15, 1946, two days after his seventeenth birthday, but more than year — to Joe's disappointment — after World War II ended. Joe's unit, the 7750 PEC Guard Company, served in Germany as part of the occupation forces, until it was demobilized in April 1948. The army honorably discharged Joe on April 19, 1948, but part of the discharge included a requirement that he enlist in the army reserve. Joe, not yet twenty, returned to his parent's home on 2nd Street. He married Alvina Garza, and the couple had a daughter, Linda Marie Gomez. All three lived with his parents, while Joe worked a series of odd jobs. He thought — wrongly — that his days as a soldier were behind him.

After World War II ended, the United States and the Soviet Union agreed in 1945 to divide the Korean peninsula at the 38th parallel. In 1947, the U.S. Joint Chiefs decided that Korea wasn't strategically valuable, and the Truman administration proposed turning Korea over to the United Nations, but the communists refused to recognize the U.N.'s authority. On January 1, 1949, the United States recognized President Syngman Rhee's Republic of Korea. The Soviets responded by creating the Korean Democratic People's Republic. On June 8, 1950, North Korea's leaders issued a manifesto calling for elections across Korea — in both the north and the south. The elections would create a Korean Parliament that would convene no later than August 15, 1950, the fifth anniversary of Korea's liberation from forty years of occupation by Japan. Ominously, the manifesto said the legislature would convene in Seoul, the capital of the U.N.-backed Republic of Korea. America and other countries paid little notice of the manifesto.

On June 25, 1950, to the shock of the Western world, ninety thousand North Korean troops invaded South Korea. U.N. Secretary General Trygue Lie described the North Korean invasion as a "war against the United Nations." U.S. President Harry Truman later recounted his immediate reaction: "If the communists were permitted to force their way into the Republic of Korea without opposition from the free world, no small nation would have the courage to resist threats and aggression by stronger communist nations. If this was allowed to go unchallenged, it would mean a third world war." General Dwight D. Eisenhower told reporters: "We'll have a dozen Koreas soon if we don't take a firm stand." The U.N. Security Council—during a Soviet boycott of the council—voted 9–0 for an "immediate cessation of hostilities" and a return north of the 38th Parallel by the North Korean forces. On June 27, Truman ordered the U.S. Far East Command to furnish naval and air support to South Korea, and, on July 7, the U.N. placed U.S. General Douglas MacArthur in command of all U.N. forces. North Korea ignored the U.N. actions and continued its invasion of South Korea, overrunning much of the nation. By mid-July, South Korean and U.N. forces had been driven to the extreme southeast end of the Korean Peninsula, in the Pusan area.

The first two weeks of September 1950 resulted in some of the heaviest fighting and casualties of the war. Truman ordered thousands of marine, navy, and army reserves back to active duty. Joe Gomez was called back into active service on September 26 and assigned to the 38th Infantry Division. He was sent to New Jersey for training, but for a time it looked like his division might not be needed in Korea. Instead of being swept into the Sea of Japan, U.N. forces—aided by immensely superior air power attacking North Korean's extended supply lines—turned the tide. On September 15 MacArthur's forces executed one of the great military maneuvers in history—the marine corps landings at Inchon. At about the same time the U.S. Eighth Army in Pusan broke the North Korean encirclement and advanced north. Seoul was recaptured and the North Korean army was routed. Only about twenty-five thousand North Koreans escaped back across the 38th Parallel. It was a "military miracle," President Truman cabled MacArthur. "I salute you all, and say to all of you from all of us at home, 'Well and nobly done.'" The U.N. forces had liberated South Korea and all but destroyed the North Korean Army.

On September 27, 1950, the U.S. Joint Chiefs of Staff told McArthur his primary objective was the destruction of all North

Korean military forces and his secondary mission was the unification of all of Korea under Syngman Rhee, if possible. The Joint Chiefs also ordered MacArthur to determine whether Soviet or Chinese intervention appeared likely. MacArthur told Washington: "I regard all of Korea open for military operations." Truman, with the U.N.'s blessing, ordered MacArthur's troops to cross the 38th Parallel. Truman's experts dismissed as a bluff Chinese Foreign Minister Chou En-lai's warnings that China would intervene if the U.N. crossed the boundary separating the two Koreas. On September 29, Secretary of Defense George Marshall sent MacArthur a personal communication informing him that he was free to cross the 38th Parallel.

MacArthur met with Truman on Wake Island on October 15, 1950, and the famous general told the president he expected formal resistance to end around Thanksgiving. MacArthur predicted that the North Korean capital, Pyongyang, would fall shortly, and he hoped to have the U.S. Eighth Army back in Japan by Christmas. The general assured the president that the Chinese would not attack, saying: "The Chinese have no air force. If the Chinese try to get down to Pyongyang there will be the greatest slaughter." He predicted that the U.N. could be holding unification elections across Korea right after the first of the year. MacArthur said there would be no need for occupation forces: "Nothing is gained by military occupation. All occupations are failures." Victory celebrations took place in the United States, and Joe Gomez wondered if he'd missed another war. But he would get his chance. While Truman and MacArthur conferred at Wake, 120,000 veteran Chinese troops already were inside North Korea.

Mao Tse-tung, chairman of the Chinese Communist Party, said publicly on October 1, 1950: "The Chinese people will not tolerate foreign aggression and will not stand aside if the imperialists wantonly invade the territory of their neighbor." Premier Chou En-lai asked the Indian government to relay this message to Truman: "If the United States, or United Nations forces cross the 38th Parallel, the Chinese People's Republic will send troops to aid the People's Republic of Korea. We shall not take this action, however, if only

South Korean troops cross the border." U.S. Maj. Gen. Charles Willoughby, head of Far East military intelligence, issued a report that said, in part: "Recent declarations by CCF [Communist Chinese] leaders, threatening to enter North Korea if American forces were to cross the 38th Parallel are probably in the category of diplomatic blackmail." Truman and the U.S. and U.N. leadership ignored Chinese warnings. On October 7, a U.N. army comprising mostly U.S. and South Korean troops crossed the 38th Parallel. On the same date, the United Nations sanctioned the reunification of Korea under Rhee's government. On October 12, the Chinese People's Republic sent troops from Manchuria across the Yalu River into Korea. The Chinese Fourth Field Army, six hundred thousand strong, had been gathering undetected on the Korean-Chinese border since June.

U.N. forces captured North Korea's capital on October 19, and between October 20 and 24, the U.S. Eighth Army and X Corps advanced north toward the Yalu River, the Korean-Chinese border. The first major U.N.-Chinese engagement took place November 1 when the U.S. 1st Cavalry Division was ambushed at Unsan. On Friday, November 24, the day after Thanksgiving, the Chinese surprised the Eighth Army along the Chongchon River, and two days later the Chinese Army, in temperatures as low as twenty degrees below zero, attacked the 1st Marines and the Army's 7th Division at the Changjin Reservoir. Historian Michael J. Varhola wrote: "When the 260,000 soldiers of the Chinese People's Volunteer Army struck near the end of November, it was in numbers and with a fury that came as a complete surprise to the largely unprepared American, South Korean, and other allied forces. U.N. commanders paid for that lack of preparation with the blood of their men and a humiliating defeat." MacArthur messaged Washington for help: "This command . . . is now faced with conditions beyond its control and its strength." He said the Chinese were intent on the "complete destruction" of his army.

In response, during a prepared statement issued at a November 30 press conference, Truman said, "We shall intensify our efforts to help other free nations strengthen their defenses . . . we shall rapidly increase our military strength." But, under questioning from reporters, Truman shook the world when he said: "There has always been active consideration of its [atomic bomb] use. . . . It is one of our weapons." United Press issued a bulletin: "President Truman said today that the United States has under consideration use of the atomic bomb in connection with the war in Korea." The Associated Press said Truman would allow his military commanders — implying MacArthur, who had publicly advocated using the atomic bomb — to decide if they needed to drop the atomic bomb. Leaders across the world said they feared Soviet intervention, World War III, and possible nuclear holocaust. The *London Times* editorialized that Truman had "touched upon the most sensitive fears and doubts of this age." Great Britain's prime minister made an emergency flight to Washington to talk to Truman. The *Times of India* ran the Truman story with a front-page banner headline: "NO NO NO." Meanwhile, MacArthur urged the U.S. to drop thirty to fifty atomic bombs on Chinese cities, but Truman's chief biographer wrote: "That choice was never seriously considered. Truman simply refused to 'go down that trail.'" Under the massive Chinese onslaught, the U.N./U.S./South Korean troops retreated.

Back home, near panic set in over the prospect of World War III and nuclear holocaust. On December 15, 1950, Truman issued a declaration of a national emergency, imposed wage and price controls, and called for still greater defense spending. In addition to calling out the troops, Truman appointed the head of General Motors in charge of a new Office of Defense Mobilization, and persuaded retired General Dwight Eisenhower (who had become president of Columbia University) to return to active duty as supreme commander of NATO. In a radio address, Truman urged every citizen to "put aside his personal interests for the good of the country."

In Korea, the battered U.N. forces established a defensive line at the Imjin River south of the 38th parallel, and on Christmas Eve — instead of heading home — the U.N. forces withdrew from North Korea. About 105,000 U.S. and South Korean military personnel and some 100,000 Korean refugees fled the besieged North

Korean port city of Hungnan aboard U.S. Navy ships. Hungnan's port facilities were then blown up and much of the city was set afire. On Christmas Eve, "with the coastline a mass of flame and billowing dark smoke," the U.S. and its allies fled North Korea, leaving the Chinese and North Koreans a clear path to recapture Seoul. The U.N. forces created a defensive line at the 37th Parallel. "We were," wrote Truman's secretary of state, George Marshall, "at our lowest point." Defeat, humiliation, war, sacrifice — perhaps even Armageddon — loomed. "Now, at Christmastime," wrote one historian, "a new wave of apprehension swept over the American people. . . . The people could not remain indifferent in the face of incessant newscasts . . . Millions resolved to enjoy one last Christmas before the deluge."

Before he was shipped overseas, Joe Gomez earned a brief leave to go home for Christmas. Amid the national gloom, the trip turned into a personal and family tragedy. Joe, his mother, and other family members drove to Pontiac, Illinois, to visit his brother, Bob, in the state reformatory. Ice and wind-whipped snow covered narrow state highway 116 between Peoria and Pontiac. An oncoming car lost control and careened toward the Gomez car. Raul, at the wheel, braked and tried to pull the Gomez car out of harm's way, but instead their car skidded and spun on the ice. Joe's mother — sitting in the back seat on the passenger side — handed Joe's baby daughter, Linda, to Joe, who was sitting on the driver's side. The two cars collided, and the passenger side of the Gomez car took the full brunt. Joe's mother, Amanda Gomez, died. Others in the car suffered cuts and bruises. Baby Linda survived, thanks to her grandmother's last-second heroics. Family photos show bandaged, grieving family members — including Joe in his uniform — standing over his mother's open coffin. Shortly after the funeral, Joe took a train back to Camp Kilmer for shipment to Korea. "We were all very sad," said Joe's brother, Raul.

On January 24, 1951, Joe and his Company K of the 38th Infantry arrived in Korea. Allied troop strength climbed to a quarter million, facing some three hundred thousand Chinese and North Korean soldiers. On January 25, U.N. forces resumed their offensive with Operation Wolfhound followed by Operation Killer, and Operation Ripper. The U.N. forces, including Joe Gomez, reached the Han River—the southern edge of Seoul—on March 7. The mission: recapture Seoul, the South Korean capital. Joe and the other American and allied solders "went through Seoul, and reduced it block by block. When they were finished, the massive railroad station had no roof, and thousands of buildings were pocked by tank fire. Seoul was conquered for the fourth time in a year. Of Seoul's more than one million souls, less than two hundred thousand still lived in the ruins." Joe received his first purple heart in the battle for Seoul, and was hospitalized with shrapnel and gunshot wounds. His brother said Joe should have been sent home, except the war got even hotter, and the generals needed soldiers back on the line. The army command ordered the walking wounded back to the foxholes, and Joe Gomez returned to combat.

On April 11, Truman relieved MacArthur of command, angering many who thought him a military genius and the Free World's best hope of defeating worldwide communism. The *Chicago Tribune* declared, in a front-page editorial, "President Truman must be impeached and convicted. His hasty and vindictive removal of General MacArthur is the culmination of a series of acts which have shown that he is unfit, morally and mentally, for his high office. . . . The American nation has never been in a greater danger. It is led by a fool who is surrounded by knaves." The Joint Chiefs of Staff supported Truman, and although congressional hearings ultimately vindicated the president, the furor over MacArthur's firing "spread confusion and increased doubt about the war in Korea."

The war went on. The Chinese and North Korean armies were determined to once more capture Seoul. Through the remainder of March, April, and May, the U.N. forces held a 140-mile defensive line —the "No-Name Line"—just north of Seoul and just south of the 38th Parallel. The U.N. line ran along the crest of a huge hill mass in East Central Korea that separated the Hongchon and Soyang rivers. Joe's unit defended Hill 800—dubbed by soldiers "Bunker Hill"—just below the 38th Parallel, and about thirty miles north and slightly west of Seoul. Supplies came from ten miles away over a single-lane dirt road that followed the Hongchon River. Bunker Hill rises six-teen hundred feet above the end of the road, and all supplies, tools and weapons were hand-carried to the top. Three rifle companies — including Joe's — defended the hill.

Headquarters assigned Joe's rifle company, King Company, to the very peak of Bunker Hill. Lieutenant Colonel Wallace M. Hanes ordered his men to build deep bunkers. Intelligence reports said the Chinese likely would strike at Bunker Hill in overwhelming numbers. "If it is necessary," Hanes told his officers, "I don't want you to worry about calling in the [friendly] fire. All you have to do is fix up your bunkers so that you will have a clear field of fire to your front and your neighbors' bunkers and won't get hit by your own shell fragments when I call down the fire." More than seven hun-dred civilians hauled supplies up Bunker Hill. While the GIs dug twenty-three deep bunkers, civilians hauled up 237,000 sand bags, 385 rolls of barbed wire, and tons of materials used for mines and other munitions. Thirty-two oxen brought up heavy 4.2-inch mor-tars and mortar ammunition. Each man, including Joe Gomez, was issued extra ammunition and twenty hand grenades. Joe's unit erected two barbed-wire aprons, one stretching along three sides at the base of Bunker Hill, the other about two hundred yards beyond.

The first two weeks of May were quiet, and the men complained that the deep bunkers were unnecessary. Then, on May 16, some 137,000 Chinese and 38,000 North Korean soldiers began moving against the No-Name Line. On the night of May 17, a patrol of Joe's unit confronted heavy Chinese opposition. Company K commander Capt. George Brownwell moved his headquarters nearer the front, but failed to bring his forward artillery observer to the new head-quarters. At about 9:30 P.M., amid a cold mountain fog, K Company heard Chinese bugles sound. Chinese soldiers were crawling up the hill. Long columns of Chinese soldiers "chanted and grunted and sang, after the manner of all Chinese at work or on the march, until the hills were hideous with their noise," wrote one historian.

At the very top of Bunker Hill, "Company K held its fire until the enemy reached the second wire barrier," wrote an official army historian. "Instead of moving frontally, the leading Chinese had slipped around to the west, cut the barbed wire in front of the 1st Platoon, and crawled up the steep part of the hill. . . . The Americans opened fire with rifles and machine guns, and tossed grenades down the hill. Quickly, Company K came to life, the action spreading in both directions like a grass fire." The commanding officer tried to call in artillery, but couldn't contact his observer because the Chinese had cut the company's communication lines. Chinese soldiers overran Company C, to the east of Joe's position. Under intense fire, a green lieutenant with nearby M Company ordered his men to retreat, opening a breach in the line. Then an enemy artillery shell landed squarely on the command post bunker, knocking out Company K's radio. Without communications and surrounded by Chinese soldiers on both flanks, Joe's unit "crumbled quickly" and retreated in disorder. The Chinese had captured Bunker Hill.

At the base of the hill, Brownwell, two lieutenants, and a sergeant frantically organized a counterattack. They gathered thirty-five men, including Joe, to retake Bunker Hill. The counterattacking force included a machine-gun crew, two men with Browning Automatic Rifles, and six riflemen, including Joe. Brownwell tried without success to obtain artillery fire, then decided to wait no longer. According to the official army report:

> [T]he 35-man skirmish line started forward, the men firing steadily and walking erect under the supporting rifle and machine-gun fire. . . . The enemy fired back with two machine guns—one of their own and one Company K had abandoned. . . . Both sides used American white phosphorous grenades of which there was an abundant supply. . . . As Company K's attack progressed, the men threw one or two grenades into each bunker they passed. . . . At the moment of a grenade burst the hill and the line of infantrymen stood out prominently in the eerie white light. The first white phosphorus grenade thrown by the enemy landed at one end of the skirmish line. The entire line stopped momentarily. One man fell dead with a bullet through his neck."

The counterattack progressed steadily, "moving a yard or two with each grenade burst. As the line reached the highest part of the hill, a grenade burst revealed three Chinese 15 to 20 feet ahead, kneeling side by side in firing position. . . . Half a dozen men (Americans) fired at once. At the same time, a Chinese whistle sounded and when the next grenade exploded two of the Chinese had disappeared. The third, still kneeling, was dead. . . . Enemy opposition diminished suddenly and then, except for a few rifle shots, ended."

The battle for Bunker Hill was savage. On the morning after the battle, American soldiers found the bodies of 28 Chinese soldiers at the top of the hill, and 40 to 50 more bodies along the barbed wire in front of the hill.

By 1:30 A.M., May 18, 1951, Company K once again controlled Bunker Hill. But Joe Gomez had been shot. According to witnesses, he was placed on a stretcher and carried to the base of the hill, then placed on the front of a Jeep (another injured man was in the back seat) and taken to a M.A.S.H hospital. He died ten days later. Nineteen days later, his wife and parents were notified of Joe's death. His official army file said: "During a counterattack launched by his company . . . Private Gomez, with complete disregard for his own safety, assaulted enemy positions in the face of point-blank small-arms and automatic weapons fire. In a final assault under intense enemy fire he fiercely charged the enemy with fixed bayonet, repulsing him with heavy losses and clearing the position. The gallantry displayed by Private Gomez reflects great credit upon himself and his military service." On September 28, 1951, the U.S. Army awarded Pfc. Joseph Gomez the Silver Star, posthumously.

Joe's brother Raul thinks Joe deserved more. "What he did, helping take Bunker Hill, was worthy of the Medal of Honor," Raul said. During the desperate battle and its aftermath, Raul said, no one recorded Joe's last moments. No one paid much attention to another private getting killed. Without better documentation of Joe's actions at Bunker Hill, Raul said, the army can't recommend Joe for the Medal of Honor. Raul has written scores of letters trying to get eyewitness accounts of Joe's heroism, but his last minutes are lost in the fog of war. "They didn't give out many Silver Stars to Mexican American privates, so you know he died heroically," Raul said. "He used to love to charge up Billy Goat Hill to drive off the enemy. When the army in Korea needed someone to charge up Bunker Hill, they had the right man. Joe Gomez was a tough, heroic fighter who loved America."

CHAPTER THIRTEEN

Last to Die

*Greater love hath no man than this, that a man lay down his life
for his friends.*
—John 15:13

B illy Goat Hill dominated 2nd Street, and the boys of Little
Mexico dominated the hill—by day a pyramid of the sun, by
night a pyramid of the moon. From the peak, the boys could see
most of their world—the thirty or so little houses and converted
boxcars turned into homes that lined unpaved 2nd Street, the rail
yard where most of them were born and where their fathers worked,
the state mental hospital looming on the northern horizon and, in
the distance, the banks of the Mississippi River. Late at night, the
boys sat around a fire, sang old Mexican songs, and talked about
going to war. They couldn't wait.

Johnny Muños was thirteen when the World War II began, and
wanted to join the older boys atop the pyramid. He wanted to hear
them sing, and talk of girls, boxing, and war. One night, he and his
best friend, Ray Alonzo, crept up the hill and hid just outside the
flickering firelight. Then they were spotted, and the older boys started
to chase them away. "Wait," said one of the older boys. "Maybe they

can get us beer." They gave Johnny and Ray an old jug and some coins, and told them to go to the nearest tavern and say they wanted to buy beer for their fathers. If they returned with beer, Johnny and Ray could stay atop the pyramid, watch the fire dance, and listen to the music and the talk of war. "So we took this big old empty beer jug down to the tavern and told the bartender we were buying the beer for our dads," Ray Alonzo recounted many years later. "The bartender was easy, and sold us the beer — but he wouldn't have sold to older boys. Then we took it back up the hill — Johnny and I were beer runners. As a reward, the older boys would let us stay, and they'd even give us a sip of beer. We heard how everyone wanted to go to war. We wanted to go, too." Johnny was too young for the World War II, but prime for the "Forgotten War."

Johnny's parents, Isabel and Victoria Muños, owned a small farm near Irapuato, Guanajuato, in central Mexico when Villa's and Obregon's armies fought each other there in 1917. Son Joseph "Big Joe" Muños recounted his parents' history: "Dad dug a hole in the floor of the house, and when they saw soldiers coming they'd hide their food in the hole, cover it with a mat, and have the children sit on the mat. 'We have no food for you,' Victoria told the soldiers. 'We have no food for our children.' Soon, the lie became true — there was no food for the four children." And, Isabel faced getting drafted into one of the armies. "Dad didn't want to get killed," added Big Joe. "In those days, either side could grab you and you couldn't do a damned thing — except leave for the United States." The family fled north in 1916, crossing into the United States at Laredo, Texas. "Two of my brothers died on the trail," said daughter Mary Muños Ramirez. "I don't know what from, but one must have caught it from the other." A Texan befriended the family, built a small wooden casket and buried both boys somewhere north of Laredo. "Mama told me the story, but she didn't know where her sons were buried — just someplace in Texas."

Isabel heard there was work at the Silvis yard, and the family headed for Illinois. The 1922 depression put pressure on Mexicans to return home, and Victoria Muños was homesick — so the family returned to Irapuato only to find that the family's house and farm had been ransacked and robbed of all valuables. "Dad said he couldn't make a living, and wanted to go back to Silvis," Mary said. "It was a bad time for mom — she was pregnant with me, but agreed to return to the United States. When they returned, the Bellman family welcomed the Muños family to share their boxcar in the first, or west, yard. A short time later, Mary was born, Victoria's ninth child.

The Muños's family fortunes quickly improved. The railroad gave the family their own boxcar, and Victoria's final three children were be born in Moline Public Hospital. Victoria gave birth to Johnny Muños on April 3, 1928, the family's eleventh child. Two months after Johnny's birth, Herbert Hoover accepted the Republican nomination for president, saying: "We in America today are nearer to the final triumph over poverty than ever before in the history of any land. The poorhouse is vanishing from among us." Instead, the Great Depression loomed.

When, in the summer of 1929, city officials relocated Little Mexico from the rail yard to 2nd Street, some of the families had money to buy or build homes. But Isabel had no savings, so he and friends hauled the family boxcar through the yard, across the tracks and over Silvis's main street to a lot at 124 2nd Street. Over the years, the family made additions and sided the house but, some eighty years later, the Muños's old boxcar still stands at 124 2nd Street. "At its heart, it's still a boxcar," said Joe Muños.

As the Mexicans moved, the world economy was crumbling. October 24, 1929, was "Black Thursday" with panic pushing stock market sales to a record decline. October 29 was "Black Tuesday" with 16,410,000 shares sold in panic selling. On November 13 — just over a year since Hoover's election — the *New York Times* index of industrial stocks fell to 224, losing half its value in just over two months. In 1930, 1,350 banks failed, and some 5 million people in the United States were unemployed. On December 11, 1931, the New York Bank of the United States collapsed — the largest of 2,293 U.S. banks to suspend operations in 1931. Another 1,493 U.S. banks collapsed in 1932.

The Chicago and Rock Island Railroad — Isabel Muños's employer—hung on for dear life, cutting pay, hours, staff, and other expenses. "All along the lines of that great system, rolling stock was stored in side tracks, the paint scaling from the onslaughts of sun and rain. Rust gathered over the rails that led to closed-down industries. Locomotives were stored on weed-grown spurs," wrote one historian. On June 7, 1933, the Rock Island Railroad filed for bankruptcy. Johnny Muños was five when his father was laid off. "We lived on relief—on charity, like everyone else," said Johnny's younger brother, Joe. "Dad hated it. He didn't like taking charity. He hated it. We wanted a job. He was a good worker. He hated taking relief—but he had a family to feed." Isabel took whatever work he could find. Public works projects were started to give jobs to the unemployed—but in 1931 Illinois passed a law that only U.S. citizens could have those jobs. Isabel was a Mexican citizen.

Foreign workers were blamed for high unemployment rates. An immigration official in Michigan wrote: "The elimination of such a large number of alien laborers . . . will work a tremendous benefit not only on the economic situation . . . but will remove from the economic field a group that for some unknown reason is able to get first consideration in employment in the industries of this country and by their removal the opening in industry will be left for residents and citizens of the United States." Some half-million Mexicans were repatriated to Mexico in the early 1930s. In Chicago, Mexican nationals wrote the Mexican counsel asking for help before "they died of starvation and cold."

Isabel and Victoria Muños kept their family in Silvis and struggled for survival. Their family was—as President Franklin Roosevelt said of one-third of the nation—"ill-housed, ill-clad and ill-nourished," but they hung on. "Everyone in the neighborhood helped each other," said Joe Muños. "We were all family, all brothers and sisters. If one house had food, everyone in the neighborhood would eat." Big Joe Muños's godfather, Eduviges Sandoval, never lost his job with the railroad, and his wife, Angelina, made sure there were always beans and tortillas enough for their neighbors and friends, the Muños. "When mom got sick, she [Angelina] helped us a lot. She made sure we got fed."

In May 1936, John D. Farrington, the Rock Island Railroad's new chief operating officer, toured the entire Rock Island system. Historian William Edward Hayes painted this picture: "Forlorn men in overalls stood by silently while Farrington walked through shops and roundhouses, asked questions and made notes. . . . The farther he went the more grim became the thin line of his mouth, the more determined the jut of his big chin. Challenge? Farrington hadn't, prior to this tour, guessed at the half of it." Farrington ordered a huge system-wide scrap metal drive. He issued an order: "Get everything on the system that can be salvaged in the way of steel and timber sorted and classified so that this material can be put to good use." Farrington used the proceeds to buy new heavy-duty rail, and rebuild thousands of miles of roadway and hundreds of sagging bridges. The railroad was hiring again, and Isabel Muños went back to work. As war raged in Europe and Asia, America's economy and railroads came back to life. When the Japanese struck Pearl Harbor, the railroads became part of the first line of national defense.

Even though six boys he knew from 2nd Street were killed in World War II, Johnny still dreamed of the day he could go to war. But on May 7, 1945 — just a month after his seventeenth birthday — Germany surrendered. At noon, Aug. 15, 1945, Japanese Emperor Hirohito went on Radio Tokyo to announce the nation's surrender. The younger 2nd Street boys who missed the war were disappointed. But the nuclear age had dawned, and the Cold War between the capitalistic Western nations and the communist Eastern Bloc meant that conflict would continue in some form.

After graduating from East Moline High School, Johnny worked for International Harvester at the combine assembly line in East Moline. On July 4, 1949, Johnny and his friends went to watch a baseball game near Galesburg, Illinois. Also in the stands that day was Mary Louise Beserra, an aspiring professional singer. Johnny and Mary met and talked and watched the sun go down and the stars come out. Near midnight, they watched fireworks. "It wasn't very long, and they were in love," said Ray Alonzo. "He started spending all his time with her." Alonzo said Johnny often drove the forty-five

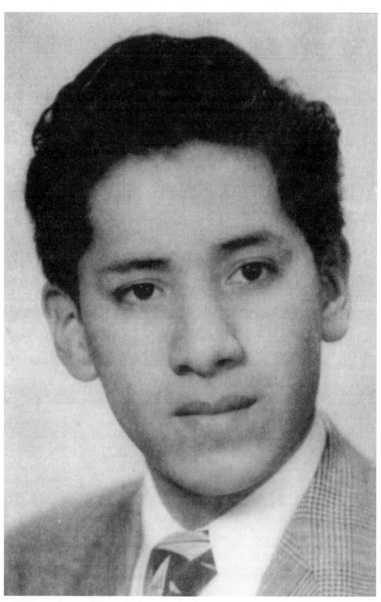

Johnny Muños

miles to Galesburg in his 1940 or '41 Chevy, and he went to the supper clubs where Mary sang. The couple loved to dance. They started talking about marriage and having a family.

Then North Korea stunned the world by invading South Korea and capturing Seoul and most of the Korean peninsula. The tide turned on September 15, 1950, when U.S. Marines landed at Inchon and recaptured Seoul. That same day, Johnny received his draft notice from the U.S. Army. He and Mary decided to marry before he went overseas, and on October 21, 1950, they wed. In January 1951 — after the Chinese Army entered the war and dealt the U.S. and U.N. forces a humiliating defeat — Johnny left for basic training at Ft. Leonard Wood, Missouri. The army assigned him to Company F of the 38th Regimental Combat Team, 2nd Infantry Division, and, after accelerated boot camp, Johnny's unit headed to Korea. The army hadn't "wasted much time getting me to this lousy hole. . . . This place isn't fit for a dog," Johnny wrote to his friend Tanilo "Tony" Soliz. In a letter dated August 13, Johnny complained of living on C rations for thirty-one straight days and sleeping on the ground. He wrote that he wished he could see Tony, a barber, because he badly needed a haircut.

In mid-summer, 1951, the war had been fought to a stalemate, with some 750,000 Chinese and North Korean soldiers dug in against some 500,000 U.N. and South Korean troops. On June 23, 1951, the Soviet delegation to the U.N. proposed a truce. On June 30, 1951, U.N. supreme commander General Matthew Ridgeway radioed his willingness to discuss truce terms with the Chinese and North Koreans. Peace talks ensued, but little progress was made toward achieving a cease-fire. On August 17, South Korean army units assaulted a previously unnamed height that would ever after be known as Bloody Ridge. "While Bloody Ridge had little strategic value," wrote historian Michael Varhola, "operations to take it were intended to both keep U.N. forces in fighting trim and to keep pressure on the enemy in order to influence the armistice negotiations." On this ridge of little value, the North Koreans and Chinese soldiers were dug in deep, and the South Koreans suffered heavy casualties. The South Koreans took Hill 940, only to be driven from

it on August 25. On August 27, 1951, American forces counterattacked in force, with artillery firing nearly a half million shells in
support. The ridge turned into a "flaming hell of whining steel and
searing flame. The trees were splintered to stubs, and fresh earth
gaped." In this maelstrom of fire and violence, while fighting for a
place of no strategic value, Johnny died—one of 740 Americans lost
in the Battle of Bloody Ridge. His body was never found. His sister,
Mary, said that two buddies reported that Johnny took a direct hit
from an artillery shell. "His body was blown apart," she said. Johnny
was listed as MIA-BNR—missing in action, body not recovered.
"There was nothing left to recover," his sister said.

"I hoped for the longest time that he'd been taken prisoner,"
said childhood friend Ray Alonzo. "I hoped for the longest time
that Johnny would come home, that someday he would just be here
again." His widow waited years before re-marrying. Isabel and Victoria received Johnny's Purple Heart, and a framed gold star to
hang in their window—the eighth star on 2nd Street. A cease-fire
was signed at Panmunjom, Korea, on July 27, 1953, but the war was
never formally ended. Johnny's name is carved in marble in Hono-
lulu, and his name can be found at a memorial at the military
cemetery at the Rock Island Arsenal.

Joe Gomez and Johnny Muños were among the 33,629 Americans soldiers and airmen—and one of more than 2 million humans
—killed in the three-year-long Korean Conflict. The truce set the
border between North and South Korea back to the 38th Parallel,
the same border as before the war, and the same border that exists
today. President Dwight Eisenhower said after the truce was signed:
"The war is over, and I hope my son is coming home soon." But two
sons of 2nd Street in Silvis, Illinois, never returned home from
Korea.

CHAPTER FOURTEEN

Homecomings

The battle's over and peace is all around you,
Sleep soldier boy sleep on.
The canon's roar can never more disturb you,
Sleep soldier boy, sleep on.
— "Sleep, Soldier Boy" (V.F.W. memorial song)

Frank Sandoval would have celebrated his twenty-eighth birthday on September 5, 1948. But instead of a fiesta, his family prepared for his funeral — and his third burial. Frank died in June 1944, in Burma, and his fellow soldiers buried him there while the battle still raged on. The army disinterred his body and reburied him in a U.S. military cemetery in India. Then, in the summer of 1948, the army disinterred him again, and shipped him back across the Pacific Ocean to the U.S. mainland. A train carried him to the Rock Island Railroad terminal in East Moline in September 1948.

A black hearse and a military escort met his train at the East Moline station. The hearse with the casket aboard drove to Silvis and made a mournful trip up 2nd Street, past Billy Goat Hill and four other homes displaying framed gold stars. American flags waved from nearly every house, and neighbors from throughout

Little Mexico, wearing their Sunday best, lined the unpaved street. Frank's childhood friends — some wearing their World War II uniforms — carried his flag-draped coffin up thirteen wooden steps from the street to the Sandoval's front door at 187 2nd Street. Then the pallbearers hoisted Frank up another flight of stairs to the house's main room. For three days family, friends, and neighbors paid their respects.

Funeral vigils in Little Mexico were "big events," said Tanilo Sandoval, Frank's younger brother. "The kids liked them because the women made all kinds of pastries, and at midnight they served hot chocolate — a real treat. The men would take a little nip and then maybe another. The women and children ate pastries and chocolates. Some people would stay up all night at the wake." Frank had died more than four years earlier in Burma, so the vigil, while somber, wasn't grim. For some, it was an excuse for a big party. "Except for mom. She acted like Frank had just died," Tanilo said. "It was hard on dad and the rest of us, but really hard on mom."

After three days of vigil, pallbearers took the casket back down the stairs and loaded it back into a hearse, which carried Frank's body two blocks to the Our Lady of Guadalupe Roman Catholic Church on 4th Street. Father L. A. Wojciewchoski conducted the funeral mass in Latin. Then Eduviges and Angelina made their first of many trips to the U.S. Military Cemetery on Arsenal Island. Mourners followed the hearse through Silvis, East Moline, and Moline, and then across a bridge over the Mississippi River to Arsenal Island. Full military honors followed: three volleys from a firing squad, four uniformed flag-bearers holding the American flag over Frank's casket as it was lowered into the grave. A bugler played taps. Soldiers carefully folded the American flag. Then an officer in full dress uniform handed the flag to Angelina and Eduviges and told them: "The government presents to you this flag under which he served." The soldiers snapped to attention and saluted.

The army returned Sgt. Claro Solis' body to 2nd Street in October 1948. Solis was first buried in an American military cemetery in Belgium after he was killed in the Battle of the Bulge in January 1945, but in the summer of 1948 his body was disinterred and shipped home.

The same ritual was enacted: Three days of vigil at the family home, lots of visitors, tears, pastries, chocolate and late-night nips of liquor. Then came the funeral mass at Our Lady of Guadalupe Church and interment. His burial plot was three away from the Sandoval brothers' graves. His family began a still-unresolved fight over whether his grave marker should be spelled Solis or Soliz. Based on his baptismal records and copies of his own signature, the army used Solis (as did the author); but the Hero Street Monument Committee, which includes four of his nephews, spelled his name Soliz on the monument erected on Hero Street.

In December 1948, the army shipped Joseph Sandoval's body home. Rain and snow disrupted his return. The city of Silvis still hadn't paved 2nd Street, and the street was too muddy for the hearse to drive from 1st Avenue (the town's main street) to the Sandoval home. So, friends carried the coffin all the way up the street, past Billy Goat Hill and to his home at 187 2nd Street, where his mother and father awaited him. Neighbors lined the street and a single soldier in full dress uniform followed the pallbearers as they lifted Joe from the hearse and carried him up the street. At the front door, they were met by Angelina and Eduviges. "It was a very sad scene," said Tanilo Sandoval. "Mom never got over the pain." During the three days of visitation "everybody but mom had some fun," Tanilo said. Just before Christmas 1948, pallbearers lowered Joe's casket into a grave next to brother Frank.

In early 1949, the army disinterred Tony Pompa's body in Italy and shipped it home. Five years had passed between Tony's death and the return of his body. His wife had remarried, and her new husband had adopted Tony's son, Tony Jr., and daughter, Sharon. So when the army contacted her about his body, she asked that Tony be shipped not to her, but to Tony's parents in Silvis.

The army knew him as Tony Lopez, and there was no easy way to change the records to his real name. He'd gone into the army as Tony Lopez, gotten married as a Lopez, was father of two children named Lopez. When the army recovered his body, his dog tags identified him as Sgt. Tony Lopez. His family and friends protested, but Tony was buried on a bitterly cold day in January 1949 in the

The Sandoval house. Photo by Marc Wilson.

cemetery on Arsenal Island under the name Tony Lopez. "We filled out all kinds of paper work and talked to everyone we could, but he was buried out there for a couple of years under the wrong name before they agreed to change his name, paperwork, and grave marker to Tony Pompa," said his younger brother, Frank.

Peter Masias came home last. The army disinterred his body and shipped it home in August 1949. His mother, Epefania, had died the previous year, so his stepfather, Agapito, hosted a three-day vigil. Neighbors said he found the vigil an excellent excuse to drink. Peter, too, was buried at Arsenal Island with full military honors.

"Behind the sound and fury of the battle about which correspondents write are the . . . graves registration boys who gather up the dirty, bloody bodies and haul them away in trucks like loads of wood to some American cemetery in Europe. . . . For no one can waste time with the dead, except to bury them in the hastiest and most simple way possible," wrote army captain Orval Faubus. The Graves Registration Service, under the command of the U.S. Army Quartermaster Corps, faced the challenge of recovering the bodies of the 286,959 Americans killed in World War II. At the end of the war, there were 359 American military cemeteries containing the remains of 241,500 World War II dead. The Graves Registration Service went to great lengths to find missing Americans, and of the 40,467 missing soldiers, 18,641 bodies were found by March 31, 1946. But Willie Sandoval wasn't one of them. Willie's father, Joseph, never fully accepted his son's death, and lack of a Christian burial. In the 1960s, Willie's brother Oscar, traveled to Holland and had his picture taken next to the cross-marked grave of an American soldier. He told his father that the grave was Willie's. Joseph Sandoval finally found closure. After his father died, Oscar Sandoval admitted that he'd lied to ease his father's mind — he hadn't found Willie's grave.

Joseph Gomez's body came home from Korea as part of the U.S. military's Operation Glory. The Graves Registration Division disinterred over 14,074 bodies from Korea, shipping them via army transport ships through Moji Port in Japan, and then on to the United States. His final resting place also is at the U.S. Military Cemetery at Arsenal Island.

Johnny Muños' body was never recovered from Korea. "There was nothing left to recovered," said his sister, Mary Muños Ramierz. "He was blown to pieces." The body of an unknown soldier was recovered from Korea and buried at the Tomb of the Unknown Solider at Arlington National Cemetery on Memorial Day, 1958.

The grief at the home of Angelina and Eduviges Sandoval seemed unending. Santiago "Yatch" Sandoval was the youngest brother of Joe and Frank Sandoval, who died in action in World War II. In 1952, the U.S. Army drafted him for service in Korea. "My mother was illiterate, but she did everything she could, contacted everyone she could to try to keep Yatch from getting drafted and sent to Korea," said Tanilo Sandoval, Yatch's older brother by three years. "She put up one heck of a fight, and lots of officials tried to help her because she'd already lost two sons in combat." But all Angelina's efforts failed, and Yatch was sent to fight in the Korean War.

Grim news arrived in the middle of 1952. The U.S. military no longer used boys on bicycles to deliver telegrams about death and injury to relatives—instead the telegrams were delivered by taxi cab. Driver Tom Pomeroy of Buddy Boy Cab Co. of Moline delivered a telegram to Angelina and Eduviges saying Yatch had been injured in combat. The telegram offered no details. "It was our fifth telegram," said Tanilo. "We got one when Frank was killed, one when Joe was injured, one when Joe was missing in action, and one when Joe was declared dead. Then we got the one about Yatch." A month or so later, the family received a letter from Yatch saying he was okay. A shell had exploded on top of his bunker, and he had been wounded, but not badly. He was awarded the Purple Heart.

The army discharged Yatch Sandoval in the spring of 1953. Just five weeks after he returned home, he and four friends crashed a vehicle on nearby Barstow Road, just east of the Rock Island rail yard. The car went off the road in the middle of the night, high centered in a ditch and flipped over, pinning Yatch.

"My brother Eddie woke me and said, 'Our brother has been killed in a car wreck," Tanilo said. "He had a really big funeral. He had lots of friends, and everyone came to the wake and the church. Mom was so afraid of him going to war, then he came back and was just back five weeks when he got killed." Santiago "Yatch" Sandoval was twenty-four. Because he was a veteran, his body was buried at the U.S. Military Cemetery at Arsenal Island, not far from his older brothers, Frank and Joe.

For the rest of their lives, Angelina and Eduviges made regular trips to the cemetery to place flowers on their sons' graves. They didn't own a car and never learned to drive, so it fell to surviving son Tanilo to take them to the cemetery every Memorial Day, Veteran's Day, and on the boys' birthdays. "To the day she died in 1984, she cried every time she visited the graves. Dad always bought flowers until he died [in 1964], and so did I." After Angelina died in 1984, "it became my job to take flowers to my brothers' graves," Tanilo said.

On Memorial Day 2007, Tanilo brought flowers to his brothers' graves for the sixtieth consecutive year. Speeches were made, the Gettysburg Address was recited, and bands played patriotic songs — but eighty-two-year-old Tanilo Sandoval listened from a distance. He sat on a folding chair in the middle of the cemetery, surrounded by the tombstones of unknown soldiers, Medal of Honor winners, his childhood friends, and his brothers Frank, Joe, and Yatch.

CHAPTER FIFTEEN

Blackballed

I have a dream that my four little children will one day live in a nation where they will not be judged by the color of their skin, but by the content of their character.
— Dr. Martin Luther King Jr.

In the summer of 1953, just as negotiators agreed to a cease-fire in the Korean War, Ray Alonzo and other veterans from Little Mexico played baseball at the ball fields on the western edge of the Rock Island rail yard. After a hotly contested game on the torrid July afternoon, Ray and three of his friends wanted something cold to drink, so they walked into the nearby Silvis V.F.W. Post 1933, at the corner of 1st Street and 11th Avenue. The bartender, an elderly, eye-patch–wearing veteran of World War I, cheerfully served the ballplayers a round of cold beer. The bartender had an idea. "You guys ought to join the post."

He explained that the Veterans of Foreign Wars of the United States was formed by an act of Congress in 1936 as a non-profit organization for current or former members of the U.S. armed forces. To be eligible for membership, the bartender said, they needed proof of overseas military service — such as an overseas expeditionary medal, a Combat Infantryman Badge, a Combat Action Ribbon, a Korean Defense Service Medal, a Navy Deterrent Patrol Insignia, hostile fire-imminent danger pay records, or proof of thirty consecutive days of duty in Korea after June 30, 1949. "I bet you boys all have at least one of those," the bartender said. They did, and they were patriots — and they cherished the idea of recreating the camaraderie they'd found when they served in the military. They'd earned their stripes as Americans. Or, so they thought.

Alonzo, who was born in 1927 while his family lived in a boxcar in the rail yard, served in the Army of Occupation in Germany after World War II. Al Lopez and Danny Razzo served in the U.S. Navy during the Korean War. A fourth ballplayer — Tanilo Sandoval — was a veteran of the U.S. Army. But Tanilo hadn't served overseas, so wasn't eligible for V.F.W. membership — even though his two older brothers, Frank and Joe, had been killed in action in World War II.

Alonzo and his friends talked. The beer at the post was cold and cheap and the location was great — just behind the ball fields and six blocks or so from Little Mexico. The fellowship with former soldiers, marines, and sailors who'd served overseas would be great. The bartender gave them applications, and Alonzo, Lopez and Razzo took them home. They returned the forms with documentation of their overseas military service. "We'll let you know real soon," the bartender promised.

Then they waited.

"A couple of weeks passed, and we heard nothing, then a couple more weeks passed and we still heard nothing," Alonzo said. Alonzo went to the Silvis post and met with its commander, Harry Crowder. Crowder said their applications had been voted on — and rejected. The Mexican American veterans had been blackballed. Crowder said the members were afraid "the Mexican Americans would take the post over because there were so many of us," Alonzo said. Crowder suggested that because there were so many, the Mexican American veterans should form their own post.

There was some anger — "but we got over it. We were used to it. We didn't like it, but we were used to it," Alonzo said. "Instead of getting mad, we decided to form our own post. We didn't want to fight. We wanted to belong." The Mexican American veterans found they needed twenty-five members for a V.F.W. charter. That was no problem. "We signed up over sixty pretty fast," Alonzo said. The national V.F.W. approved a new post, No. 8890, on May 28, 1954, based in neighboring East Moline. At first, Post 8890 met in members' homes or in local taverns. Then Post 8890 rented a former American Legion Hall above and next to the Majestic Theater in downtown East Moline. In 1972, Post 8890 moved to its own two-story building — a former church building — on 1st Street in East Moline. As of 2007, Post 8890 had over one hundred members and is active in the Silvis and East Moline communities.

"One of our great missions — maybe the mission that keeps us strong — is to keep the memory of Hero Street, U.S.A. alive," said Alonzo. Frank Pompa, brother of hero Tony Pompa, is a past commander of 8890. "The post means a lot to us as Mexican American veterans — but we welcome all American veterans to join us, or just visit," Frank said. The post was named Ibarra-Gomez Post 8890, in honor of two western Illinois men who died earning silver stars in Korea — Michael Ibarra of Milan and Joe Gomez of 2nd Street Silvis. "There was talk about naming the post in honor of my brothers — Frank and Joe — but they [post organizers] asked my dad [Eduviges Sandoval], and he didn't want any controversy. He told them: 'Let them rest in peace,' " Tony Sandoval said.

Meanwhile, the white-only Silvis V.F.W. Post 1933 faded away. As membership dwindled, Post 1933 sold its building, and began meeting periodically and then sporadically at local restaurants and taverns. In 2006, Silvis Post 1933 voted to close and consolidate with Moline Post 2153 — even though the East Moline post was several miles closer. The Silvis post likely would have survived had it allowed the Mexican Americans into membership. An old Chicago, Rock Island and Pacific Railroad caboose now stands on the location of the former Silvis V.F.W. post, just south of the once-mighty Rock Island rail yard.

"I was pretty sore when we got blackballed," Alonzo said. He said the Mexican American veterans never complained to state or national V.F.W. officials. "A couple of years later [after the blackballing], some of the higher-ups in the V.F.W. learned what happened and were pretty upset and apologized to us. I guess it took me many years to get over it. But the wound finally healed." Despite the blackballing, Alonzo said he thinks the V.F.W. is a "great organization." He was elected three times to be commander of V.W.F. Post 8890—the last time in 2007.

"Sure, if the Silvis Post had let us in, they would have been a better, stronger post," Alonzo said. "Maybe they'd still be around if they'd let some new blood in. We would have been good members —very good members. But that was a long time ago, and there are no hard feelings. We're sorry for them that they had to close their post."

CHAPTER SIXTEEN

Thank God, Paved at Last

*These three long [war] years of suffering and pain and hardships
and heartaches have taught me how to be tolerant and . . . patient.
I have seen poverty and cruelty and I want to place myself above
both of them. I do not seek to fight unless it is completely right."*
— Dr. Hector Garcia, founder of the American G.I. Forum

Angelina and Eduvigues Sandoval buried three sons in the U.S.
Military Cemetery at Arsenal Island. Three times, "Taps" was
played for their sons, and three times military salutes were fired
over their boys' graves. Three times, uniformed U.S. soldiers folded
and handed Angelina and Eduviges American flags and offered the
grieving parents thanks from a grateful American government. But
after the ceremonies — after the echoes of "Taps" and the rifle
shots had faded — Angelina and Eduvigues were still Mexicans living in the United States. "Their sons fought and died for America,
but every January until they died mom and dad had to register with
the federal government as legal aliens," said their son, Tanilo.
"They'd lived here most of their lives and given their sons to the
United States, but they were still, in the end, just old Mexicans living
as aliens in America."

It wasn't just the old Mexicans who'd lost sons who felt left behind. When Mexican American veterans returned home after World War II, they once again faced bias, prejudice, and bigotry. In the Midwest, wrote one historian, "restaurants, bars and barbershops refused service to Mexicans. Public baths were off limits to them, and most theaters had restricted seating." Overseas, Hitler and Mussolini were dead, the death camps closed, and Japanese imperialism eradicated. During the war, Mexican Americans found equality when they shared foxholes with American GIs of all backgrounds. Their scars, Purple Hearts, and other medals attested to their patriotism. They'd been treated as Americans when they fought and died in Europe, Asia, and the Pacific, but when the Mexican American veterans came home, they often found themselves to still be second-class citizens. Even the Veterans of Foreign War post in Silvis denied them admission. They had little to no voice in government and few services. Their streets in Little Mexico remained unpaved. "I tell you, it's a damn shame. All the boys die and they won't even fix our street. We get no more respect than a dog," Joseph Sandoval, father of slain paratrooper Willie Sandoval, said in 1970.

Progress was made on some fronts. Wartime labor shortages had broken employment color barriers as Mexican Americans finally landed good jobs at the federal government's Rock Island Arsenal, and at the manufacturing plants run by John Deere, International Harvester, and Caterpillar. The plants quickly retooled from military production to meet soaring demand for domestic farm implements. And, in 1948, the Chicago, Rock Island and Pacific—long the main employer for Little Mexico's residents—came out of fifteen years of bankruptcy. The railroad converted the Silvis shop from steam engine to diesel locomotive technology and built a fifty-track hump-retarder yard in Silvis. Nobody had trouble getting a good job.

Younger Mexican Americans escaped the yard, getting cleaner, better-paying jobs at the Arsenal or the farm implement plants. In addition to better jobs, the Mexican American community began moving into better homes, and more of their children performed better in school, and some went to college. Still, 2nd and 3rd Streets in Silvis, the heart of Little Mexico — where the refugees from the revolution still lived — remained unpaved, and the area politically powerless. "Nothing ever seemed to change there, except the kids moved out when they got the chance," said Tanilo Sandoval.

Mexicans faced discrimination nationwide, and a few leaders began seeking change. The spark of the Mexican American civil rights movement occurred in Texas where discrimination against Mexicans and Mexican Americans was perhaps the worst in the nation. In Texas, restaurants, stores, and public swimming pools denied service to Mexican Americans. In Illinois, when the army returned the bodies of Frank Sandoval, Claro Solis, Joe Sandoval, Tony Pompa, and Peter Masias to Silvis in 1948 and 1949, they were accorded full military honors and burials at the U.S. Military Cemetery at Arsenal Island. But in Texas, army Pvt. Felix Longoria received much different treatment when his body was shipped home to his hometown of Three Rivers. Japanese gunfire cut down the twenty-six-year-old Longoria in June 1945 while he was on a patrol in Luzon, the Philippines. When the army disinterred his body and sent it home in 1949, the Rice Funeral Home, the only funeral home in Three Rivers, refused use of its chapel for Longoria's funeral. "The whites just won't like it," funeral home owner T. W. Kennedy told Longoria's widow, Beatrice.

She asked for help from Dr. Hector Garcia, president of the newly founded American GI Forum. Garcia had founded the GI Forum in Corpus Christi in 1948 to help Mexican American veterans who were being denied benefits due them under the G.I. Bill of Rights. Garcia called the funeral home to plead Longoria's case, asking Kennedy: "But in this case the boy is a veteran, doesn't that make a difference?" Kennedy responded: "That doesn't make any difference. You know how the Latin people get drunk and lay around all the time. The last time we let them use the chapel, they got all drunk and we just can't control them."

Garcia then sent seventeen telegrams to officials saying: "The denial [of funeral services] was a direct contradiction of those same principles for which this American soldier made the supreme sacrifice in giving his life for his country and for the same people who now deny him the last funeral rites." The telegram asked for "immediate investigation and correction of the un-American act." Only one official responded, Lyndon B. Johnson, who'd just been elected to the U.S. Senate from Texas in one of the closest and bitterest races in state history. He telegrammed Garcia: "I deeply regret . . . the prejudice some individuals extend even beyond this life. I have no authority over civilian funeral homes. Nor does the federal government. However, I have today made arrangements to have Felix Longoria buried with full military honors in Arlington National Cemetery here at Washington where the honored dead of our nation's war rest." Johnson's telegram also said, "This injustice and prejudice is deplorable." Beatrice Longoria responded to Johnson that she was "humbly grateful for your kindness in my hour of humiliation and suffering." Longoria's burial in Arlington took place on February 16, 1949, with LBJ, Lady Bird Johnson, and President Truman's military aide present. The episode birthed a relationship between the American G.I. Forum and the future president that would finally lead to the paving of 2nd Street in Little Mexico. The episode also launched the American GI Forum into the role of being the largest Mexican American civil rights organization in the country with chapters in twenty-eight states. One of the chapters was in Moline, Illinois, about five miles from Little Mexico.

In Texas, signs said: "White Trade Only." Signs in Silvis said: "We reserve the right to refuse service to anyone." Area taverns wouldn't serve Mexicans or Mexican Americans. The Silvis V.F.W. Post and Eagles Club maintained Anglo-only memberships. There wasn't an overt color barrier, "but we knew where we weren't welcome," said Tanilo Sandoval. For many years, Little Mexico's residents typically turned the other cheek, formed their own clubs, stayed to themselves, and asked little of the government. "Our culture was like the indigenous civilization which teaches stoicism. We were taught to perform and not gripe about a tough life," wrote Margarito Soliz, nephew of slain World War II soldier Claro Solis. Soliz was one of many who decided change was needed.

Silvis' 1st Ward runs from 7th Street to 2nd Street (1st Street is a non-residential thoroughfare that serves as the border with East Moline).Little Mexico's residents rarely voted, and city, state, and Rock Island County officials largely ignored the area. But unrest was rising in Little Mexico. The American G.I. Forum urged Mexican Americans to learn the U.S. government system and become involved in elections. Two lifelong friends from 4th Street in Little Mexico — Joe Terronez and Nick Trujillo — began organizing the residents of Little Mexico.

Terronez and Trujillo read the rules and gathered the official forms, then helped Little Mexico's residents apply for citizenship and register to vote. "They needed to speak English, and to know the name of the president [to become citizens]," Terronez said. "They needed photos — we gave them rides to the photographers and money for photos if they needed it. Then we gave them rides to the federal courthouse in Rock Island, where they were sworn in as citizens. One day we took nineteen people in at once, and they all became American citizens the same day!"

The increase in registered voters finally gave Little Mexico political clout and, in 1959, Soliz won election to the Silvis City Council. He was college educated (and ultimately would earn a Ph.D), but city hall shunned him, and the other seven council members routinely opposed or ignored any plans he proposed. After one term on the council, Soliz stepped aside in favor of Terronez, a self-admitted "tough character" who wouldn't be bullied. "The Solizes were artists, musicians, and teachers," Terronez said. "I was better prepared to stand up to the Anglos."

Terronez's preparation began in the rail yard, where he was born in 1929 — perhaps the last child born there. Shortly after his birth, his family moved to 147 4th Street, where his parents — Benito and Felisa, refugees from Mexico's Revolution — raised thirteen children. "My dad was a blacksmith at the yard. He was a great worker. Somehow, all of us always had food to eat — and food for anyone else who was hungry, even the hobos during the Depression," Terronez said.

In elementary school, Terronez made friends with an Anglo student. "He invited me over to his house after school. That was a big deal — we didn't usually mix with Anglos. He was an only child, and his parents were both college-educated teachers with jobs. They had everything — radios, a washing machine, carpets, and pictures hanging on the walls, towels, furniture and a refrigerator full of food. I was stunned. I was a kid from a house with parents who couldn't read who were raising thirteen kids in the middle of the Depression. I looked around at everything and said to myself: 'This is all possible. In America you can have things.' And from that day forward I wanted to be successful, and have things and give things to my mother and father and brothers and sisters. I saw the American Dream and wanted part of it. That visit changed my life." In school, Joe studied as hard and long as possible — especially anything related to civics, history, and government. "I wanted to know how the system worked — how America worked, so I could be part of it," Terronez said.

After graduating from East Moline High in 1948, Terronez began working for International Harvester's plant in East Moline. He was a hard worker, made friends easily, and rose within the United Auto Workers union hierarchy. He served as a union steward, then won election to the full-time job as grievance arbitrator. "I learned a lot from the union," he said. "I learned how to be tough and not get pushed around. I learned you'd better not let your own people get away with things, because all of us would be hurt. Mostly, I learned how to get things done the right way, and that I didn't have to take nothing from nobody, if it wasn't right." When he was elected alderman in 1963, Terronez was ready, willing, and able to fight City Hall — by knowing and using the rules. "I didn't care if they liked me, so long as they learned to respect me and treated my people right."

City residents approved a general obligation bond in 1965 to pave and repave all city streets — all but 2nd Street. "They said the houses [on 2nd Street] were built all over the place and on the right-of-way, so there was no real street there and no way to get a straight street that could be paved," Terronez said. All other streets were approved for paving, including 3rd Street in Little Mexico. But after the city had paved all the streets except 3rd Street, city officials said they'd run out of money—so there'd be no paving for 3rd Street either. Councilman Terronez went to the next city council meeting and said the city had no choice—3rd Street had been part of a general obligation bond that the public had voted on. "I screamed discrimination out loud. This was during the height of the Civil Rights movement and they caved in and found the money to pave 3rd Street." That left 2nd Street—the street of eight dead heroes—as the only unpaved street in the city.

Terronez, the Moline Chapter of the American GI Forum, V.F.W. Post 8890, and the local American Legion Post took up the cause of 2nd Street. They all started talking up the history and the heroism of the eight men from 2nd Street who'd died in combat. Moline Dispatch reporter Vi Murphy began telling the story of the street's sacrifices, and Chicago newspapers spread the story. Terronez persuaded the City Council in 1967 to officially change the name of the street to Hero Street, U.S.A. The U.S. Post Office honored the name change request, and new street signs were erected. But still the street, grand name and all, renamed unpaved. The situation angered people—including some who were very powerful and had connections with the president of the United States.

Vicente Ximenes grew up in Floresville, Texas, thirty miles south of San Antonio. Out of some one hundred Mexican Americans who started together in elementary school in Floresville, Ximenes was one of only five to graduate with the high school class of 1939. He entered the University of Texas at Austin in 1940, where he became friends with medical student Hector Garcia. During World War II, Ximenes served in the U.S. Army Air Force, flying fifty missions as a bombardier on B-17s in North Africa and winning the Distinguished Flying Cross before retiring as a major. After the war, he earned bachelor and masters degrees in economics at the University of New Mexico and became active in the American GI Forum, which his friend, now Dr. Hector Garcia, founded after the war. He and Garcia actively worked for the election of John Kennedy and Lyndon Johnson as president and vice president in the 1960 election. After Kennedy's assassination, President Johnson appointed Ximenes to be deputy director of the Agency for International Development in Panama in 1966. In 1967, Johnson appointed Ximenes to be commissioner of the U.S. Equal Employment Opportunity Commission, and appointed Ximenes to chair a cabinet committee on Mexican American Affairs. Ximenes became friends with Robert C. Weaver, the first black secretary of Housing and Urban Development. They were front-line warriors in LBJ's so-called War on Poverty.[10]

Another warrior was Jesse Perez, a retired navy chief petty officer, who became commander of the nearby Moline chapter of the American GI Forum in the mid-1960s. Perez was born in Moline after his parents fled to Illinois during the Mexican Revolution. He said he told the story of 2nd Street in Silvis, Illinois, to Ximenes during a national convention of the American GI Forum. Ximenes took a personal interest in helping the veterans of Little Mexico receive credit for their heroism. "He was a very powerful man, and he cared about Hero Street. When we needed help, he was there for us," said Terronez.

Ximenes visited Silvis in 1968. "He walked the street and talked to everyone, and went inside their homes. And we all talked about building a park to honor the heroes," Perez said. The park didn't come easily. Ximenes helped arranged a $44,450 matching grant from the U.S. Department of Housing and Urban Development to finance a memorial park on Hero Street. But, Perez said, the city didn't want the park and balked at providing the matching money — or even signing the contract needed to build the park. At the outset, the council was 7–1 against the park, with only Terronez voting in favor. That's when the American GI Forum intervened.

Perez visited Silvis City Hall and chatted with Mayor Bill Tapman, who only voted if the council tied. Silvis had applied for a federal grant for a city water system. Perez offered Tapman the help of the American GI Forum's office in Washington, D.C. "I told him he might need our help, but he didn't think so. Then he went to Washington to try to get the federal money. He called me at home at about ten at night and said I was right, the city would need the forum's help." Tapman agreed to support the Hero Street Park.

(*Left to right*) Jesse Perez, Lt. Col. D. H. McClinton, Vicente Ximenes, and Joe Terronez

The city council then voted 5–3 to support the Hero Street Park. A short time later, the federal government approved funding for the Silvis water project. "We were very well-connected in Washington, and we knew how to get things done," Perez said. "We knew how to get things done in Silvis, too." The city borrowed half of the half — a $22,663.67 loan from the Bank of Silvis. The rest of the matching funds came from in-kind donations of equipment, labor, and supplies. John Deere Co. donated the use of heavy equipment, and volunteers, including members of V.F.W. Post 8890 and the GI Forum, did manual labor to complete the grant requirements. John Deere Co. also assigned one of its engineers — Joe's cousin Tony Terronez — to work full time on the park.

Ximenes gave the first annual Memorial Day address at Hero Street Memorial Park in 1969. He said of the heroes: "If they died for democracy, they did not die so that darker Americans would continue to face barriers in education and employment. . . . They did not die so that thousands of Americans, brown, black, yellow or white, should suffer the pangs of starvation and malnutrition. They did not give their lives so that comfortable Americans should begrudge aid and assistance to those who have not had equal opportunity. They did not die so that Mexican Americans, Negroes, and American Indians should fail to receive acknowledgement of a job well-done through equal promotions, training opportunities and good wages."

The new park and the attention from Johnson Administration officials prompted the city to pave Hero Street. "At first, they used the old excuse that there wasn't a proper right-of-way, not enough setbacks," said Terronez. "But we told them we'll have people from all over the country coming to see Hero Street Memorial Park, and it would be embarrassing to the city and its residents if the street wasn't paved. So they finally agreed to pave it." Silvis' other streets were paved with funding from general obligation bonds repaid by all citizens, including those living on unpaved 2nd Street. But when it came time to pave Hero Street, the city council chose another option. The city contributed $30,000 from its motor fuel tax fund, and levied a $26,000 special tax against only the residents of Hero

Street, U.S.A. "Change came slowly, and there was none at first, but once men have served their country — and their friends have died for the country — change had to come," said Ray Alonzo. Added Terronez: "When I gave speeches I always liked to say: We showed the world. Color and all that don't mean anything. We're not second-class citizens. We are first-class Americans!"

Epilogue

No World War II veterans live on Hero Street, U.S.A. any longer. Louis Ramirez, who guided us through the prologue of this book, died in August 2008 just a couple of weeks before his 90th birthday. In April 2007, another of the street's World War II servicemen, navy veteran Robert "Big Bob" Muños, died. He was the older brother of Private Johnny Muños, who was killed in Korea. This left Anthony Soliz, older brother of hero Claro Solis, as the oldest surviving veteran from Hero Street at age 91. As of August 2008, he lived alone in a second-story apartment in Davenport, Iowa. He gave up his part-time janitorial job at age 90.

The Chicago, Rock Island and Pacific Railroad, the company that brought the Mexican refugee settlement to Silvis, entered its third and final bankruptcy in 1975. Protracted efforts to reorganize or merge into the Union Pacific failed. A bankruptcy court ordered liquidation in mid-January 1980, and the last train ran on March 31, 1980, after 129 years of operations. The National Railway Equipment Co. operates what is left of the yard. The company repairs diesel locomotives from all around the world. The roundhouse, red boxcars, family gardens, and much of the old tracks are gone.

The Silvis School District built a new elementary/junior high school on 5th Street in the 1960s, and abandoned McKinley School. After part of the old school burned, the rest of the building was torn down. Today, only the steep concrete front steps remain.

Our Lady of Guadalupe Church, which was born in the rail yard, outgrew its building on 4th Street and moved to 17th Street. It annually holds one of the area's largest festivals celebrating Latino heritage. Many of the families of the heroes still belong to the church.

V.F.W. Post 8890 in East Moline struggles as its members die. Ray Alonzo is serving his third term as post commander. "We can't get any new blood." The post's bar, which is run by Frank Pompa, younger brother of Tony Pompa, is open Wednesdays through Saturdays. It's the best place to find memorabilia about Hero Street, U.S.A.

The city of Silvis works hard to maintain Hero Street Memorial Park on old Billy Goat Hill. Each year, the crowds at the Memorial Day celebrations seem to dwindle. The Soliz brothers — Frank, Sonny, Tony and Guadalupe — and others led a successful, if erratic, effort to erect a war memorial at the intersection of 1st Avenue and Hero Street, U.S.A.

Tanilo Sandoval, brother of heroes Frank and Joe Sandoval, places hundreds of little American flags at the monument every Memorial Day, July 4th, and Veterans Day. Tanilo lives nearby in East Moline and visits Hero Street at least once a day. He is the street's historian and best guide.

Joe Gomez's house at 181 Hero Street burned down years back and was never rebuilt. Standing on the empty lot provides a good view of Hero Street. Across the street, and about half a block to the left, is the home of Willie Sandoval. Almost directly across is the home of Tony Pompa, which has a marker saying "childhood home of Tony Pompa." Looking to the right, one sees the little home of Claro Solis, then, farther to the right, the former boxcar home of Johnny Muños. The old shack that was Peter Masias's home has been replaced. On the same side of the street as Gomez's lot stands the old two-story house that Eduviges Sandoval had built in 1929. Old-timers say they can still picture Angelina and her daughters out near the street washing clothes. Others say they can still hear her sobs.

Eduviges and Angelina are buried side-by-side in the St. Mary's Cemetery, two miles away from their home, and about one hundred yards from the grave of their baby son, Norberto. Eduviges died on Veterans Day, November 11, 1967, at age 81. Angelina died in 1984, just short of her 88th birthday. She was quoted in the *Chicago Today* newspaper on November 1, 1971, saying, through a translator: "I don't understand why there always has to be war. I hate to think that some day my grandchildren will have to go, too." Their graves are on a treeless, east-facing hill, and in the dead of winter — when the trees beyond the hill are bare — the view reaches the old train yard in Silvis. Eduviges' name is misspelled — Edubigus — on his gravestone. And his first name is followed by the initial "M" — which his son, Tanilo, says is inexplicable. "The funeral home did it," he said, with a shrug.

Joe Terronez served twenty-eight years on the Silvis City Council, including the last four as mayor, the first Hispanic mayor in Illinois. "I know where every water and sewer pipe is in the city," he said. "I never missed a council meeting or a committee meeting. I worked hard for my people, and for all the people of Silvis." Joe, who was born in 1929, lives in a house he built some fifty years ago on 3rd Street. He helps organize the annual Memorial Day celebrations at Hero Street Park. He maintains voluminous records on the history of the street and its people. Joe's nephew, Jeff Terronez, was elected as State's Attorney for Rock Island County.

The children of the heroes — Joe Sandoval's sons Mike and Henry Sandoval, Joe Gomez's daughter Linda, and Tony Pompa's children, Tony Jr. and Sharon — never knew their fathers, and rarely, if ever, return to Hero Street, U.S.A. Willie Sandoval's nephew, Brandon Alfonse Sandoval, graduated from the U.S. Air Force Academy in 2006.

Joey Soliz great-nephew of Claro Solis, who died in the Battle of the Bulge, remains close to Hero Street. "I think of all the sacrifices my grandfather and his generation made to get here from Mexico, and how fortunate I am and my children are to be Americans. My folks tried to get me to go to Mexico with them," Joey added, "but I opted not to go at that time. I thought I'd feel out of place, not being *Mexican enough* to speak the language."

Joey took a trip to Texas several years ago with his step-son, Chris, and a few in-laws on an all-guy vacation. "We went to a restaurant in Austin, and all the employees were Mexican. I looked in the kitchen, and the dish washer and the cooks were Mexicans. Our waiter struggled with English, and I think he was surprised that I couldn't help in Spanish. And I thought, this kid could be me. I could be him."

Joey and the guys then visited Big Bend National Park in southwest Texas, just across the Rio Grande River from Mexico. After four days in the desert, "I sat on the river bank at Santa Elaina Canyon, and looked across, and thought about my grandparents living over here, and how hard it was to cross over from Mexico to America. I thought about all the sacrifices that generation made so my generation could have what we have — so we could be Americans. I thought about my uncle dying, and the seven other guys from Hero Street [who were killed in combat]. I thought about that waiter back in Austin and the life he might have led in Mexico, his family, and the family I probably still have in Mexico. I thought about all the people on the other side and how in desperation they crossed this river for a chance at a better life. Then I felt this void for never having been there."

So Joey walked over to the river's edge, pulled off his shoes and socks, pulled his shirt over his head, and waded into the Rio Grande. The current was strong, but it was only about fifteen feet across and the water was only waist-deep. Once on the other side, peering at a fifteen-hundred-foot peak directly in front of him, he thought, "I'm now in the motherland, out in the middle of nowhere, and I've just crossed in the wrong direction." He went back to Texas, sat down on the other side, and cried.

Notes

Preface

xii   *The eight combat*   Resolutions, Illinois Legislature (Oct. 26, 1971) and Congressional Record (Nov. 18, 1983).

xii   *war years' experience*   Rivas-Rodriguez, *Mexican Americans*, xvii.

xii   *treated him like*   Letter made available to the author by Frank Soliz, nephew of Claro Solis.

xii   *When the war*   Flores, "What A Difference a War Makes"; in *Mexican Americans & World War II*, 176.

xii   *represented a distinct*   McManus, *Deadly Brotherhood*, 4.

xii   *somewhat biased against*   Ibid., 10.

xiii   *General treatments of*   Rivas-Rodriguez, *Mexican Americans*, xvii.

Prologue

3   *Loved and tender*   Fehrenbach, *Fire and Blood*. 64.

4   *The residents of*   Resolutions, Illinois Legislature (Oct. 26, 1971) and Congressional Record (Nov. 18, 1983).

6   *In 1969, city*   Documents on file with former Mayor Terronez.

7   *Our countries are*   Paz, "Mexico and the United States"; in *The Labyrinth of Solitude*, 357.

7   *Before the Mexican*   Garcia, *Mexicans in the Midwest*, 26.

7   *In 1910*   McWilliams, *North from Mexico*, 152.

7   *The war brought*   Garcia, *Mexicans in the Midwest*, 26.

Chapter 1

9   *Do we truly*   Quoted by Shorris, *Life and Times of Mexico*, 26–27.

Chapter 2

13   *Mucho trabajo*   Shorris, *Life and Times of Mexico*, 227.
14   *That day he believed*   Krauze, *Mexico*, 260.
16   *She was born*   Baptismal record provided to author by Georgia Sandoval Herrera, Angelina's daughter.
16   *one-fifth of the country*   Krauze, *Mexico*, 219.
17   *one million lives*   Miller, *Mexico*, 283–285.
17   *turned against him*   Ibid., 291.
17   *their parents' misery*   Fehrenbach, *Fire and Blood*, 465.
17   *bought and sold peons*   McLynn, *Villa and Zapata*, 35–36.
18   *In cold, damp pre-dawn*   Ibid., 153.
18   *Madero was a communist*   Fehrenbach, *Fire and Blood*, 504.
19   *instead of Madero's government*   Krauze, *Mexico*, 268.
19   *Generals Huerta and Díaz*   Shorris, *Life and Times of Mexico*, 239.
19   *Wilson wired Washington*   McLynn, *Villa and Zapata*, 156.
19   *Your husband's downfall*   Ibid., 158.
19   *He boasts of it*   Krauze, *Mexico*, 71.
20   *The assassination of Madero*   Ibid., 267.

Chapter 3

21   *It is said*   Villaseñor, *Macho!*, 39.
23   *Prisoners were routinely*   McLynn, *Villa and Zapata*, 225–227,
23   *people grew accustomed*   Krauze, *Mexico*, 364.
23   *The revolution's leaders*   Plana, *Villa and the Mexican Revolution*, 82.
24   *I proposed not*   Guzman, *Memoirs of Pancho Villa*, 349.
24   *Let us satisfy*   McLynn, *Villa and Zapata*, 235.
24   *To save on bullets*   Conaway, *Mexican Revolution*, 28.
24   *Villa dispatched*   Quirk, *Mexican Revolution*, 261.
24   *The so-called battle of Leon*   Katz, *Life and Times of Pancho Villa*, 495.
25   *had to disperse*   Guzman, *Memoirs of Pancho Villa*, 475.
25   *There are a*   Katz, *Life and Times of Pancho Villa*, 495–496.
25   *I have run*   McLynn, *Villa and Zapata*, 301.
25   *After six years*   Ibid., 338–339.
26   *1916 is remembered*   Conaway, *Mexican Revolution*, 44.
26   *There is no accurate*   Miller, *Mexico*, 283.
26   *Mexico's population declined*   Shorris, *Life and Times of Mexico*, 266.

26   *Nearly a million*   Ibid., 267.

26   *The tensions engendered*   Garcia, *Mexicans in the Midwest*, 51.

27   *American companies sent*   Ibid., 19.

27   *obtained a permit*   Herrera, Georgia Sandoval, family records.

27   *They saw many*   Urrea, *Devil's Highway*, 94.

Chapter 4

30   *Real estate brokers*   Garcia, *Mexicans in the Midwest*, 56.

32   *Mexicans were also*   Clements, *Woodrow Wilson*, 175.

32   *uniting native-born*   Sobel, *Coolidge*, 283–284.

32   *American leaders were*   Brands and Schlesinger, *Woodrow Wilson*, 133.

32   *bloody tide of lynchings*   Clements, Woodrow Wilson, 101.

32   *killing of Mexicans*   McWilliams, *North from Mexico*, 109.

32   *Heraldo of Mexico*   Ibid., 110.

33   *Calvin Coolidge succeeded*   Sobel, *Coolidge*, 4.

Chapter 5

39   *Just the year before*   Garcia, *Mexicans in the Midwest*, 42.

39   *Any idea that*   Ibid., 44.

39   *8,150 — 71 percent — walked*   Davis, *1922 . . . Strike*, chart, 67.

39   *An estimated fourteen hundred*   *Davenport Democrat*, July 7, 1922, 1.

40   *To the railroad barons*   Davis. *1922 . . . Strike*, 48–63.

40   *Lewis called for*   Angle, *Bloody Williamson*, 3–10.

41   *The railroad hired*   Davis, *1922 . . . Strike*, chart, 71–72.

41   *other Mexican workers*   Ibid., 69.

41   *have been cruelly*   Dean, *Warren G. Harding*, 119.

41   *guards began cursing*   *Davenport Democrat*, July 9, 1922, 1.

42   *Nine passengers were*   Davis, *1922 . . . Strike*, 83–85.

42   *last bulwark between*   Ibid., 87–89.

42   *Col. Frank Taylor*   *Davenport Democrat*, July 9, 1922, 1.

42   *lawlessness and violence*   Dean, *Warren G. Harding*, 118–120.

43   *president tried to mediate*   Davis, *1922 . . . Strike*, 89–90.

43   *The walkout had*   Hayes, *Rock Island Lines*, 204.

Chapter 6

45   *Not counting Mexicans*   McWilliams, North from Mexico, 97.

46   *First to be fired*   Kraut, *Records*, Series A, Part 2: Mexican Immigration, 1906–1930.

46   *cut the number*   Hayes, *Rock Island Lines*, 203.

46   *devastating*   Garcia, *Mexicans in the Midwest*, 41,
46   *Mexicans to leave*   Ibid., 42.
46   *semi-pauperism*   Ibid., 45.
47   *indigent foreigners*   Ibid.
47   *Juan Pompa was sixteen*   Family history recounted to author by Frank Pompa.
48   *work for everyone*   Kraut, *Records*, Series A, Part 2.
48   *paid as little as twelve centavos*   Garcia, *Mexicans in the Midwest*, 51.
48   *Mexicans flooded north*   Ibid., 47.
48   *conquered' people*   McWilliams, *North from Mexico*, 126.
49   *skipping school*   Carter, *Mexican Americans in School*, 41.
51   *Being an aerial*   WGN TV documentary, *Hero Street.*
51   *reminds me of Mexico*   Ibid.
51   *Conditions . . . are bad*   Turner, *War Diary*, Dec. 28, 1943.
51   *Give for a bath*   Ibid., Dec. 29, 1943.
51   *Today the 449th*   Ibid., Jan. 8, 1944.
51   *They must need us*   Ibid., Jan. 9, 1944.
51   *Falling bombs from*   Ibid., Jan. 14, 1944.
51   *dirty, tired sleepy*   Ibid., Jan. 15, 1944.
52   *Almost forgotten*   WGN TV documentary, *Hero Street.*
52   *sixty-five tons*   Turner, *War Diary*, Jan. 17, 1944.
52   *thirty-six thousand men*   Katz, *Battle for Rome*, 349.
52   *Our plane has*   WGN TV documentary, *Hero Street.*
52   *into a mountainside*   *449th Bomb Group Historical Records*, narrative report No. 19, Jan. 31, 1944.
52   *just his dog tags*   Ibid.

Chapter 7

54   *No one has been barred*   Kennedy, Message to Congress, June 19, 1963, quoted in the New York Times, June 20, 1963.
58   *toughest engineering job*   Webster, *Burma Road*, 59.
58   *ten thousand-foot passes*   Ibid., 58.
58   *Charles Monroe*   Copy of Monroe's letter given to author by Tanilo Sandoval.
59   *sick work elephants*   Webster, *Burma Road*, quotes White, 221.
60   *as viciously concentrated*   Ibid., 238.
60   *turn my guts*   Ibid., 218.
60   *wish you were dead*   Tuchman, *Stilwell*, 449–450.
61   *jungle, rain and mud*   Monroe letter.
61   *As we circled*   Kessler, *World War II*. March 2001.
61   *simply terrified*   Tuchman, *Stilwell*, 451.
61   *decimated Merrill's Marauders*   Webster, *Burma Road*, 218.
62   *outgunned and outnumbered*   Kessler, *World War II*, March 2001.

62   *Frank was killed*   Tobias letter to Sandoval family, copy furnished to author.

63   *This is most difficult*   Monroe letter.

63   *Presidential citation*   Kessler, *World War II* magazine, March 2001.

Chapter 8

65   *aliens of any race*   Garcia, *Mexicans in the Midwest*, 227.

65   *force repatriation of Mexicans*   Kraut, *Records*, Series A, Part 2.

70   *Pimps and prostitutes*   Megellas, *All the Way to Berlin*, 26.

71   *fighting on Salerno*   Breuer, *Geronimo!*, 124.

71   *We're supposed to drop*   Ibid., 127.

71   *Word that 1,300 tough Americans*   Ibid., 131.

72   *touch and go all the way*   Breuer, *Geronimo!*, 145.

72   *82nd Airborne reinforcements*   Katz, *Battle for Rome*, 48.

72   *3,950-foot Mount Sammuecro*   Breuer, *Geronimo!*, 156.

72   *constant shelling*   Megellas, *All the Way to Berlin*, 38.

73   *kill their fellow man*   Ibid., 46.

73   *54 killed in action*   Ibid., 48.

73   *paratroopers huddled*   Breuer, *Geronimo!*, 172–173.

73   *black-hearted devils*   Ibid., 173.

74   *I'm home Dad*   Family records provided to author by Al Sandoval.

74   *more men killed*   Megellas, *All The Way to Berlin*, 92.

74   *Presidential Unit Citation*   Ibid., 93.

74   *accomplished great things*   Ibid., 102.

74   *tolerably certain*   Hastings, *Armageddon*, 8.

75   *Brad and Patton*   Ibid., 31.

75   *updated their wills*   *Bridge Too Far*, 157–183.

75   *escorted by more*   Megellas, *All the Way to Berlin*, 109.

75   *Waal River at Nijmegen*   Ryan, *Bridge Too Far*, 188–189.

76   *congested with SS*   Ibid., 345

76   *Captain Delbert Kuehl*   Breuer, *Geronimo!*, 327.

76   *suicide mission*   Megellas, *All the Way to Berlin*, 136.

76   *automatic weapons and rifle fire*   Breuer, *Geronimo!*, 350.

76   *bullets were flying*   Megellas, *All the Way to Berlin*, 144.

77   *Kuehl remembered* Breuer, *Geronimo!*, 353.

77   *Germans still controlled*   Ibid., 355.

77   *There was no tactical*   Ibid., 356–357.

77   *in the slaughterhouse*   Ibid., 357.

77   *Vandervoort recalled*   Ibid.

78   *hanging by their fingernails*   Ryan, *Bridge Too Far*, 477.

78   *Three hours before*   Ibid., 479.

78   *attack could have worked*   Hastings, *Armageddon*, 49.

78   *a rotten plan*   Ibid., 57.
79   *on a combat patrol*   Megellas, *All the Way to Berlin*, 171.
79   *one missing*   Ibid., 196.

Chapter 9

81   *Defend . . . to the last*   Bayerlein, *After Action Reports*, 86.
84   *baptized Joseph Claro*   Frank Soliz provided copy of baptismal records to author.
85   *never sets if*   Solis letter made available to author by Frank Soliz.
85   *treated me like a white person*   Ibid.
85   *His letters*   Copies shown to the author by his nephew, Frank Soliz.
85   *fighting outfit*   Ibid.
85   *They gave me a gun*   Ibid.
85   *My voyage overseas*   WGN TV documentary, *Hero Street*.
86   *We were required*   McManus, *Deadly Brotherhood*, 85.
86   *eleven thousand casualties*   Reardon, *Victory at Morain*, 7–14.
86   *Panzer Lehr Division*   Bauer, *History of World War II*, 719.
87   *long duration of bombing*   Bayerlein, *After Action Reports*, 50.
87   *I don't believe Hell*   Ibid., 47.
87   *Nothing but a wooden cross*   Hastings, *Armageddon*, 92.
87   *undoubtedly the most formidable*   Ambrose, *The Victors*, 256.
88   *depleted, exhausted, used up*   Ibid., 258.
88   *next round of fighting*   Ibid., 93.
88   *Another Christmas*   Family records shown to author by Frank Soliz.
89   *average GI*   Kershaw, *Longest Winter*, 135.
89   *our outfit broke*   Hastings, *Armageddon*, 223.
89   *most dismal days*   Parker, *Battle of the Bulge*, 152.
89   *Allied air forces*   Ibid., 202–203.
89   *50 Germans fought fiercely*   Ibid., 221.
90   *their memories will die*   Faubus, *In this Faraway Land*, 452.
90   *greatest artillery battles*   Ibid., 281.
90   *other guy's armpit*   Hasting, *Armageddon*, 201.
90   *this is Patton*   Parker, *Battle of the Bulge*, 219–220.
90   *only one who was warm*   Ambrose, *Eisenhower*, 299.
91   *Death looked very inviting*   Ibid., 302.
91   *hell of a country*   Parker, *Battle of the Bulge*, 301.
91   *coldest night*   Hastings, *Armageddon*, 234.
91   *If I don't come home*   WGN TV documentary, *Hero Street*.
91   *I can see the Germans*   Ibid.

Chapter 10

93   *Every time it snows*   McManus, *Deadly Brotherhood*, 346.

94   *married her third husband*   Epifania Masias' death notice, *Davenport Daily Times*, Feb. 21, 1948. (Thanks to Roy Booker.)

98   *attended Silvis schools*   *Moline Daily Dispatch*, Aug. 9, 1949. (Thanks to Roy Booker.)

98   *standing tall*   WGN TV documentary, *Hero Street*.

98   *at least fifty push-ups*   Weber, "517th Parachute Regimental Combat Team."

99   *feverish preparations*   Breuer, *Geronimo!*, 380.

99   *England to Reims*   Ibid., 446.

99   *snow-covered fields*   Ibid., 410.

99   *greatest concentration confrontation*   Parker, *Battle of the Bulge*, 212.

99   *shells and flares*   Faubus, *In this Faraway Land*, 455.

99   *Christmas fireworks*   Ibid., 457.

99   *never capitulate*   Parker, *Battle of the Bulge*, 270.

100   *I kept from freezing*   McManus, *Deadly Brotherhood*, 60.

100   *mines and booby traps*   *139th Airborne Engineer Battalion*.

100   *prize son-of-a-bitch*   Ross, *Sky Men*, 238.

100   *cut to pieces*   Breuer, *Geronimo!*, 446.

101   *blood and flesh of their friends*   McManus, *Deadly Brotherhood*, 176.

101   *attacking battalions lost*   Parker, *Battle of the Bulge*, 287.

101   *withering enemy fire*   Parker, *Battle of the Bulge*, 301.

101   *people running everywhere*   Ross, 224.

101   *on the defensive*   Breuer, 453.

101   *six degrees below zero*   Parker, *Battle of the Bulge*, 305.

101   *turns your stomach*   McManus, *Deadly Brotherhood*, 64.

101   *great piece of fighting*   Hastings, *Armageddon*, 230.

101   *Patton struck*   Parker, *Battle of the Bulge*, 306.

102   *eighty-four minefields*   Ross, *Sky Men*, 234.

102   *cleaning up minefields*   McManus, *Deadly Brotherhood*, 74.

102   *vicinity of Flamierge*   Ross, *Sky Men*, 235.

102   *victory was costly*   Ross, *Sky Men*, 235–237.

102   *bulldozers through snow drifts*   Ibid., 244.

102   *Winston Churchill*   Kershaw, *Longest Winter*, 174.

102   *six hundred thousand men* Ibid., 174.

102   *so badly mauled*   Parker, *Battle of the Bulge*, 336.

103   *memories of the friends*   McManus, *Deadly Brotherhood*, 346.

103   *Chalons-sur-Marne*   Ross, *Sky Men*, 255.

103   *get out of the water*   Ibid., 256.

103   *17,122 American and British*   Breuer, *Geronimo!*, 541.

103   *sixty thousand troops*   Hastings, *Armageddon*, 369.

103   *to be slaughtered*   Breuer, *Geronimo!* 542.

104   *German antiaircraft*   Hastings, *Armageddon*, 369.

104   *Winds blew twenty*   Ross, *Sky Men*, 287.

104   *big steaks and apple pie*   Ibid., 284.

104   *drew a parachute*   Ibid., 285.

104   *parachute north of Wesel*   *139th Airborne Engineer Battalion.*

104   *flak so thick*   Ross, *Sky Men*, 290.

104   *air column alone*   Ibid., 297.

105   *intense ground fire*   Ibid., 296.

105   *flaming coffins*   Ibid., 297.

105   *four hundred feet*   Ibid., 297–298.

105   *We were raked*   Breuer, *Geronimio!*, 547.

105   *Trees and power lines*   Ross, *Sky Men*, 296–297.

105   *chutes never opened*   Ibid., 298.

105   *vicious firefights*   Breuer, *Geronimio!*, 548.

105   *393 men killed*   Ibid., 558.

105   *Roll of Honor*   *139th Airborne Engineer Battalion.*

106   *no doubt of success*   Ross, *Sky Men*, 320.

106   *not worth the cost*   Ibid., 321.

106   *U.S. Military Cemetery*   *Moline Dispatch*, Aug. 9, 1949.

Chapter 11

107   *died needlessly*   Ambrose, *Victors*, 330.

111   *into the hedgerows*   Reardon, *Victory at Mortain*, 11.

112   *the damnedest country*   Ibid., 10.

112   *lying wounded*   Faubus, *In this Faraway Land*, 233.

112   *fierce tank battle*   Reardon, *Victory at Mortain*, 170–171.

112   *tossed grenades*   Ibid., 216.

112   *tank and artillery fire*   Ibid., 227.

113   *Germans withdrew*   Ibid., 269–270.

113   *Presidential citation*   *41st Armored Infantry Regiment.*

113   *Dear Frank*   Letter, courtesy of Joe's sister, Georgia Sandoval Herrera.

113   *pray for me*   Ibid.

113   *Berra killed*   *41st Armored Infantry Regiment.*

114   *hit in leg*   Letter, courtesy of Georgia Sandoval Herrera.

114   *Has Hank and Mike*   Ibid.

114   *inflicted great damage*   Ambrose, *Victory*, 339.

114   *spring is here*   Faubus, *In this Faraway Land*, 578–579.

115   *Allies had agreed*   Ibid., 337–341.

115   *search the town*   *41st Armored Infantry Regiment.*

115   *started, ended in confusion*   Ibid.

115 *no communications*   Houcek, *Elbe Operation*, 5.

115 *completing the operation*   *41st Armored Infantry Regiment*.

116 *into heavy fire*   Houcek, *Elbe Operation*, 5–6.

116 *Germans were killed*   Ibid., *Elbe Operation*, 6–7.

116 *tanks took cover*   Ibid., 8.

116 *Are you kidding*   Ibid.

116 *all were exhausted*   *41st Armored Infantry Regiment*.

117 *outside bazooka range*   Houcek, *Elbe Operation*, 3.

117 *effective fighting force*   Ibid., 4.

117 *60 MIAs*   Ibid., 17–18.

117 *second purple heart*   *41st Armored Infantry Regiment*.

118 *It was very sad*   *Chicago Today*, Nov. 1, 1971, copy courtesy of Joe Terronez.

Chapter 12

119 *The Chinese have come*   McCullough, *Truman*, 815.

122 *elections across Korea*   Fehrenbach, *This Kind of War*, 3.

122 *If the communists*   quoted by McCullough, *Truman*, 776–777.

123 *if we don't take firm stand*   Ibid., 781.

123 *Security Council voted*   Ibid., 777.

123 *naval and air support*   Varhola, *Fire and Ice*, v.

123 *By mid-July*   Fehrenbach, *This Kind of War*, 9.

123 *called back to active service*   Records provided by Raul Gomez.

123 *well and nobly done*   McCullough, *Truman*, 799.

124 *Soviet or Chinese intervention*   Fehrenbach, *This Kind of War*, 181.

124 *ordered MacArthur's troops*   McCullough, *Truman*, 799.

124 *dismissed as bluff*   Ibid., 799.

124 *Marshall sent MacArthur*   Fehrenbach, *This Kind of War*, 182.

124 *the greatest slaughter*   Ibid., 185.

124 *no need for occupation forces*   McCullough, *Truman*, 803–804.

124 *120,000 veteran Chinese*   Fehrenbach, *This Kind of War*, 193.

124 *Mao Tse-tung*   Ibid., 187.

124 *If the United States*   Ibid..

125 *Recent declarations*   Ibid., 188.

125 *Chinese Fourth Field Army*   Ibid., 193.

125 *When the 260,000 soldiers*   Varhola, *Fire and Ice*, 11.

125 *MacArthur messaged for help*   McCullough, *Truman*, 816.

126 *one of our weapons*   Ibid., 821.

126 *United Press issued*   Ibid., 822.

126 *doubts of this age*   Fehrenbach, *This Kind of War*, 268.

126 *NO,NO,NO*   McCullough, *Truman*, 822.

126 *never seriously considered*   Ibid., 832.

126 *near panic set in*   Ibid., 833.

126 *defensive line at Imjin River*   Varhola, *Fire and Ice* 14.

126 *100,000 Korean refugees*   Ibid., 291.

127 *Hungnan's port facilities*   Fehrenbach, *This Kind of War,* 250.

127 *our lowest point*   McCullough, *Truman,* 833.

127 *one last Christmas*   Fehrenbach, *This Kind of War,* 254.

128 *southern edge of Seoul*   Varhola, *Fire and Ice,*15–16.

128 *two hundred thousand*   Fehrenbach, *This Kind of War,* 303.

128 *Truman must be impeached*   McCullough, *Truman,* 845.

128 *Chiefs of Staff supported Truman*   Ibid., 854.

129 *Three rifle companies*   Gugeler, *Combat Actions,* 166.

129 *Headquarters assigned Joe's*   Ibid., 168–170.

129 *chanted and grunted and sang*   Fehrenbach, *This Kind of War,* 331.

130 *cut communications lines*   Gugeler, *Combat Actions,* 172.

130 *crumbled quickly*   Ibid., 173.

131 *Enemy opposition diminished*   Ibid., 176–177.

131 *Nineteen days later*   Records provided by Raul Gomez.

131 *American soldiers found*   Gugeler, *Combat Actions,* 178

131 *During a counterattack*   Copy of Silver Star documentation provided to the author by Raul Gomez.

Chapter 13

135 *The poorhouse is vanishing*   Wilson, *Herbert Hoover,* 127.

135 *banks collapsed*   Samuelson, *Concise Encyclopedia of Economics.*

136 *Railroad filed for bankruptcy*   Hayes, *Rock Island Lines,* 219.

136 *only U.S. citizens*   Garcia, *Mexicans in the Midwest,* 225.

136 *alien laboerrs*   Ibid., 232.

136 *repatriated to Mexico*   Ibid., 238.

136 *died of starvation and cold*   Ibid., 228.

137 *Forlorn men in overalls*   Hayes, *Rock Island Lines,* 237–239.

139 *badly needed a haircut*   Letter to nephew Tony Soliz.

139 *discuss truce terms*   Fehrenbach, *This Kind of War,* 237–240.

139 *little strategic value*   Varhola. *Fire and Ice,* 23.

140 *nearly a half million shells*   Ibid.

140 *a flaming hell*   Fehrenbach, *This Kind of War,* 353.

140 *one of 740 Americans lost*   Varhola, *Fire and Ice,* 23.

140 *33,629 Americans*   McCullough, *Truman,* 935.

140 *son is coming home*   Ibid., 936.

Chapter 14

145 *Behind the sound and fury*   Faubus, *In this Faraway Land,* 567.

145 *241,500 World War II dead*   Anders, *With All Due Honors.*.

146 *Tomb of the Unknown*   U.S. Army Quartermaster Corps.

147 *Surrounded by tombstones*   The author sat with Tanilo Sandoval during the Memorial Day services. Afterward, Tanilo guided the author through the cemetery to the graves of his three brothers and many friends.

Chapter 16

152 *These three long*   *Justice for My People,* KEDT-TV.

153 *no more respect than a dog*   *Chicago Today,* Nov 1, 1971.

153 *steam engine to diesel*   Hayes, *Rock Island Lines,* 285.

154 *whites just won't like it*   Caro, *Master of the Senate,* 741.

154 *can't control them*   Ibid., 741.

155 *Arlington National Cemetery*   Ibid., 742.

155 *Truman's military aide*   Ibid., 751.

155 *indigenous civilization*   Letter to author, Sept. 19, 2003.

158 *Vicente Ximenes grew up* Martinez   Vicente Ximenes, Oral History Project.

161 *The city borrowed*   Records provided by former Mayor Joe Terronez.

161 *Memorial Day address*   Copy of speech provided to author by Joe Terronez.

Bibliography

Ambrose, Stephen E. *Band of Brothers*. New York: Touchstone/Simon & Schuster, 1992.

——. *The Victors: Eisenhower and His Boys, the Men of World War II*. New York: Simon & Schuster, 1998.

Anders, Steven E. *With All Due Honors: A History of the Quartermaster Graves Registration Mission*. Quartermaster Professional Bulletin, Sep. 1988.

Atwater, James D. and Ramon E. Ruiz. *Out from Under: Benito Juarez and Mexico's Struggle for Independence*. New York: Zenith Books/Doubleday & Co., 1969.

Bauer, Lt. Col. Eddy. *The History of World War II*. Barnes & Noble Inc., 2000.

Bayerlein, Fritz, *After Action Reports of the Panzer Lehr Division Commander From D-Day to the Ruhr*. Edited by P. A. Spayd and Gary Wilkins. Atlglen, Penn: Schiffer Military History, 2005.

Brand, H. W., and Arthur Schlesinger. Woodrow Wilson. Time Books: 2003.

Breuer, William B. *Geronimo! American Paratroopers in World War II*. New York: St. Martins Press, 1989.

Caro, Robert A. *Master of the Senate: The Years of Lyndon Johnson*. New York: Alfred A. Knopf, 2002.

Carter, Thomas P. *Mexican Americans in School: A History of Educational Neglect*. New York: College Entrance Examination Board, 1970.

Clements, Kendrick A. *Woodrow Wilson, World Statesman*. First published in 1987 by G. K. Hall & Co., reprinted by Kenrick A. Clements, Chicago, 1999.

Conaway, William J. *Mexican Revolution*. San Miguel de Allende, Mexico: Publicationes Papelandia, 2003.

Cortés, Hernan. *Letters from Mexico*. Translated by Anthony Pagden. New Haven: Yale University Press, 1986.

Díaz, Bernal. *The Conquest of New Spain*. Translated by J. M. Cohen. Baltimore: Penguin Press Ltd., 1963.

Dunn, James W. "The Ledo Road." *Builders and Fighters, U.S. Army Engineers in World War II*. Barry W. Fowle, general editor. Fort Belvoir, Va.: U.S. Army Corps of Engineers, 1992.

Faubus, Orval Eugene. *In this Faraway Land*. Conway, Ark.: River Road Press, 1971.

Fehrenbach, T. R. *Fire and Blood: A History of Mexico*. New York: Da Capo Press, 1995.

———. *This Kind of War*. New York: Macmillen, 1963. Reprinted by Brassey's, 1994.

Flynn, James R. *"The Railroad Shopmen's Strike of 1922 on the Industry, Company, and Community Levels."* PhD dss, Northern Illinois University, 1993.

41st Armored Infantry Regiment. Http:///www.2ndarmoredhellonwheels.com/units/41st.html.

Frisbee, John L. "Operation Varsity." *Valor Magazine: Journal of the Air Force Association*, March 1996.

Garcia, Juan R. *Mexicans in the Midwest, 1900–1932*. Tucson: University of Arizona Press, 1996.

Gugeler, Russell, *Combat Actions in Korea*. U.S. Army, 1954.

Guzman, Martin Luis. *Memoirs of Panco Villa*. Translated by Virginia H. Taylor. Austin: University of Texas Press, 1965.

Hayes, William Edward. *Rock Island Lines: The First Century*. Circulation Publishing and Marketing L.L.C., 1953; updated 2000.

Hashway, Thomas. *E-history of Operation Varsity*. Http:///thedropzone.org/europe/hashway.htm.

Hastings, Max. *Armageddon: The Battle for Germany, 1944–45*. New York: Borzoi Books, published by Alfred A. Knopf/a division of Random House, 2004.

Katz, Friedrich. *The Life and Times of Pancho Villa*. Stanford, Ca: Stanford University Press, 1998.

Katz, Robert. *The Battle For Rome: The Germans, the Allies, the Partisans, and the Pope, September 1943–June 1944*. New York: Simon & Schuster, 2003.

Kershaw, Alex. *The Longest Winter*. New York: Da Capo Press, 2004.

Korda, Michel, *Ike, An American Hero*, New York: HarperCollins, 2007.

Kraut, Alan M. *Records of the Immigration and Naturalization Service*. University Publications of America, 1994.

Krauze, Enrique. *Mexico: Biography of Power*. Translation by Hank Heifetz. New York: HarperCollins, 1997.

Leon-Portilla, Miguel. *The Broken Spears: The Aztec Account of the Conquest of Mexico*. Boston: Beacon Press, 1962.

Lozano, Rafael; Beatriz Zurita, Francisco Franco, Teresita Ramierz, Patricia Hernandez and Jose Luis Torres. *Mexico: Marginality, Need, and Resource at the County Level*. Http:///www.rockfound.org/Library/Challenging—Inequities—In—Health-From—Ethics—to—Action.pdf.

Martinez, Erika. *Vicente Ximenes*. U.S. Latino and Latina World War II oral history, University of Texas at Austin.

McCullough, David. *Truman*. Simon & Schuster. New York. 1992.

McLynn, Frank. *Villa and Zapata: A History of the Mexican Revolution*. New York, Carroll & Graf Publishers, 2002.

McManus, John C. *The Deadly Brotherhood*. New York: Presido Press/Random House, 1998.

McWilliams,Carey. *North from Mexico: The Spanish-Speaking People of the United States*. New edition, updated by Matt S. Meier. New York: Praeger, 1990.

Merriam, Robert E. *The Battle of the Bulge*. New York: Ziff-Davis Publishing. New York. 1947.

Megellas, James. *All the Way To Berlin*. New York: Presido Press/Random House, 2003.

Miller, Robert Ryal. *Mexico: A History*. Norman, Okla.: University of Oklahoma Press, 1985.

Newark, Tim. *Turning the Tide of War: 50 Battles that Changed the Course of Modern History*. London: Hamlyn/Octopus Publishing Group Ltd., 2001.

The 139th Airborne Engineer Battalion: Unit History. Http:///www.ww2-airborne.us/units/139/139.html.

Parker, Danny S. *Battle of the Bulge*. Originally published 1991 by Combined Books Inc.; published 2004 by Da Cappo Press.

Parkes, Henry Banford. *A History of Mexico*. Boston: Houghton Mifflin, 1960.

Paz, Octavio. *The Labyrinth of Solitude*. Translated by Lysander Kemp, Yar Milos, and Rachel Phillis Belash. New York: Grove Press, 1985.

———. "Mexico and the United States." Translated by Rachel Phillips Belash. First published in *The New Yorker*, Sept. 17, 1979. *Included in Paz's The Labyrinth of Solitude and Other Stories*. New York: Grove Press, 1985.

Plana, Manuel. *Pancho Villa and the Mexican Revolution*. New York and Northampton: Interlink Books, 2002.

Powell, Philip Wayne. *Miguel Caldera: The Taming of America's First Frontier (1548–1597)*. Tucson: University of Arizona Press, 1977.

Powell, Philip Wayne. *Soldiers, Indians and Silver*. Tempe: Center for Latin American Studies, Arizona State University, 1975.

Prescott, William H. *History of the Conquest of Mexico*. New York: Modern Library/Random House, 2001.

Rivas-Rodriguez, Maggie, editor. *Mexican Americans and World War II*. Austin: University of Texas Press, 2005.

Quirk, Robert E. *The Mexican Revolution 1914–1915: The Convention of Aquascalientes*. Indiana University Press, 1960. Reprinted Greenwood Press, 1981.

Reardon. Mark J. *Victory at Mortain*. University Press of Kansas, 2002.

Ross, Kirk B. *The Sky Men*. Atglen, Pa.: Schiffer Publishing, 2000.

Ryan, Cornelius. *A Bridge Too Far*. New York: Touchstone/Random House, 1974.

Samuelson, Robert J. *The Great Depression*. In *The Concise Encylopedia of Economics*. The Library of Economics and Liberty, 2002. Http:///www.econlib.org/library/Enc/Great Depression.html.

Sanchez, George I. *Forgotten People: A Study of New Mexicans*. Albuquerque: University of New Mexico Press, 1940.

Shorris, Earl. *The Life and Times of Mexico*. New York: W.W. Norton & Co., 2004.

Sobel, Robert. *Coolidge: An American Enigma*. Washington, D.C.: Regnery Publishing, Inc., 1998.

Steinbeck, John; edited by Robert E. Morseberger. *Zapata*. New York: Penguin Books, 1975.

Smith, Jean Edward. *Grant*. New York: Simon & Schuster, 2001.

Thomas, Hugh. *Conquest: Montezuma, Cortes, and the Fall of Old Mexico*. New York: Touchstone/Simon & Schuster, 1993.

Tobar, Hector. *Translation Nation: Defining a New American Identity in the Spanish-Speaking United States*. New York: Riverhead Books, 2005.

Tuchman, Barbara W. *Stilwell and the American Experience In China, 1911–45*. New York: Macmillan Co., 1970.

Turner, Damon A. *War Diary: 449th Bombardment Group (22 November 1943–30 June 1944)*. Http:///www.norfield-publishing.com/449th/wardiary.html.

Urrea, Luis Alberto. *The Devil's Highway*. New York: Back Bay Books/ Little, Brown and Co., 2004.

Urrea, Luis Alberto. *Across the Wire: Life and Hard Times on the Mexican Border*. New York: Anchor Books/Random House, 1993.

Varhola, Michael J. *Fire and Ice: The Korean War, 1950–1953*. New York: Da Capo Press, 2000.

Villaseñor, Victor. *Macho!* Houston: Arte Publico Press, University of Houston, 1973

Webster, Donovan. *The Burma Road*. New York: Farrar, Straus, and Giroux, 2003.

Wilson, Joan Hoff. *Herbert Hoover, Forgotten Progressive*. Long Grove, Ill.: Waveland Press, 1992.

Womack, John Jr. *Zapata and the Mexican Revolution*. Vintage Books, 1968.

———. *Rebellion in Chiapas: An Historical Reader*. New York: The New Press, 1999.

Wood, Michael. *Conquistadors*. Berkley and Los Angeles: University of California Press, 2000.

Videos

Hero Street, Busch Creative Services, Joel Kramer, executive producer; Mike Stout, director; St. Louis. 1984.

Hero Street, WGN-TV, Jim Zerkekh, Bill Borson and Pam Pearson, executive producers; Rick Thompson, director; Chicago, 1992.

Also: Public Television Station KEDT's Website, Justice for My People.com, 2007.

Military Records

"517th Parachute Regimental Combat Team: A Short History." *Airborne Quarterly*, Winter 1998.

Air Force Magazine Online. November 2000, Vol. 83, No. 11.

"Tomb of the Unknown Soldiers." *Quartermaster Review*, Jan.–Feb. 1964.

449th Bomb Group Historical Records, narrative report No. 19, Jan. 31, 1944, archived at USAF Historical Research Agency, Maxwell AFB, Montgomery, Ala.

LoneSentry.com, Division History, 17th Airborne Division. Based on *The Army Almanc: A Book of Facts Concerning the Army of the United States*. Washington, 1950: U.S. Government Printing Office.

Index

Aachen, Germany, 88

Africa, military service in: Tony Pompa (Tony Lopez), 51; Vicente Ximenes, 158; Willie Sandoval, 70

Alonzo, Ray, 133–34, 137, 140, 148–51, 162, 164

Ambrose, Stephen E., 107

Americal Division, 5

American Federation of Labor (AFL), 38

American G.I. Forum, 152, 154–55, 158

American Legion Post, 158

Anti-immigrant sentiments, 46–47

Anzio, Italy, 52, 73

Ariano, Mike, 115–17

Arlington National Cemetery, 146, 155

Arsenal Island National Military Cemetery: burials with military honors, 154; Clario Solis (Soliz), 91, 142–43; Frank Sandoval, 63, 141–42, 152; Johnny Muños, 140; Joseph Sandoval, 63, 143, 152; Peter Masias, 106, 145; Santiago Sandoval, 147; Tony Pompa (Tony Lopez), 52–53, 143, 145. *See also* Rock Island Arsenal; Unrecovered remains

Baseball, 35, 48

Battle of Bastogne, 89–90, 99–102

Battle of Bloody Ridge, 139–40

Battle of León, 24–25

Battle of the Bulge, 74, 81, 88–91, 114

Battle of the Falaise Pocket, 87

Bayerlein, Fritz, 81, 87

Beer on Billy Goat Hill, 133–34

Bellman family, 135

Berlin, Germany, 115, 117

Beserra, Mary Louise, 137, 139, 140

Bettendorf Ordnance Steel Foundry, 70

Big Bend National Park, 166

Billy Goat Hill: drinking beer on, 5, 132–34; Hero Street Memorial Park, 159–62, 164; playing war on, 119–20

Birth of a Nation, The (Griffith), 32

Bloomington, Ill., 41–42

Bolshevik Revolution of 1917, 32

Bradley, Omar N., 74–75, 86, 112

Breuer, William B., 77

Brotherhood of Railroad Carmen strike of 1922, 38–44

Brownwell, George, 129–30

Buddy Boy Cab Co. (Moline, Ill.), 146

Burials. *See* Arsenal Island National Military Cemetery

Burma Road, 58

Camp Forest, Tenn., 98

Camp Mackall, N.C., 98

Capano, John, 89
Carell, Paul, 86
Carranza, Venustiano, 23–24, 28
Carter, Thomas P., 49
Caterpillar factory, 153
Catholic Church: during the Mexican Rev-
    olution, 23; Our Lady of Guadalupe
    Church (Silvis, Ill.), 33, 37, 142, 164; St.
    Mary of Guadaloupe Church (Romita,
    Mex.), 14–15; St. Mary's (East Moline,
    Ill.), 33, 46
Chicago, Ill., 42
Chicago, Rock Island and Pacific Railroad:
    bankruptcy, 64, 163; Depression of 1921
    job losses, 46–47; Depression of 1929,
    135–36; Frank Sandoval and, 55; post-
    war employment, 153; pre-WWII recon-
    struction, 137; recruitment of Mexican
    men, 29–30, 47–48; union strike of 1922,
    38–44. See also Little Mexico rail yard
Children: growing up in "Little Mexico",
    38, 54–57, 84–85, 94–97, 107–11, 122;
    playing on Billy Goat Hill, 5, 119–20,
    132–34. See also Education; Schools
China: entry into Korean War, 124–26,
    139; immigration to the U.S., 27; Japa-
    nese invasion of, 58
China-India-Burma Theatre, 58–63
Chou En-lai (Chinese foreign minister),
    124–25
Churchill, Winston, 58, 102, 105
Civil Rights Movement, 154–56
Clark, Mark, 71–72
Clinton, Iowa, 41
Coal miner strikes, 40
Cold War, 137
Coolidge, Calvin, 33
Corey, Robert, 106
Corpus Christi, Tex., 154
Council Bluffs, Iowa, 42
Couri, Joseph, 91
Crowder, Harry, 149

Daugherty, Harry M., 43
Death and burial: along la Despolado, 28,
    47, 134; Carmen Sandoval, 68; Frank
    Sandoval, 62–63, 113–14, 120, 141–42;
    Joe Gomez, 10, 131–32, 140, 145–46;
    John & Peter Sandoval, 68; John F. Ken-
    nedy on, 54; Johnny Muños, 140;
    Joseph Clario Solis, 91–92, 114, 120,

142–43; Joseph Sandoval (son of Edu-
    viges), 63, 117–18, 120, 143; Peter
    Masias (Macias), 105–106, 114, 120,
    145; Santiago Sandoval, 146–47; Tony
    Pompa (Tony Lopez), 52–53, 114, 120,
    143, 145; Willie Sandoval, 79–80, 114,
    120, 145. See also Unrecovered remains
Decena Tragicia (Ten Tragic Days), 20
Deportation Act of 1929, 65
Depression of 1921, 39, 46–47
Depression of 1929: Hoover election as
    president, 135; neighborhood remem-
    brances of, 7; New York Stock Ex-
    change and, 120; railroad strikes of
    1922 and, 43–44; raising a family dur-
    ing, 64–68; repatriation to Mexico, 39,
    46–47, 136
Devil's Highway (la Despolado), 27–28
Díaz, Felix, 18–20
Díaz, Porfirio, 14, 16–17
Discrimination: aliens in America, 152;
    depression-era employment, 64–65;
    forced Mexican repatriation, 39, 46–
    47, 136; railroad unions, 41; in Silvis,
    Ill., 30–37; Silvis City Council, 161–62;
    toward Mexican Americans, 154–55; to-
    ward veterans, 148–51, 153
Dunbeck's drug store, 30

East Moline VFW Post 2153, 150–51
Education: Clario Solis, 84–85; Frank
    Sandoval, 57; G.I. Bill of Rights, 154;
    Joe Terronez, 156–57; Johnny Muños,
    137; Tony Pompa, 45–46, 49; Willie
    Sandoval, 65, 70
82nd Airborne Division, 70–80
Eisenhower, Dwight D., 74, 105, 115, 123,
    126, 140
Elbe River, 114–16
Evans, Lane, 5

Farrington, John D., 137
Faubus, Orval, 90, 112
Finnel, John W., 116
Fitzgerald, James, 41
Fitzgerald, James, Jr., 41
"Forgotten War," Korea as, 134
Fort Benning, Ga., 70, 98
Fort Bruning, Neb., 51
Fort Leonard Wood, Mo., 139
Fort McClellan, Ala., 111

449th Bomber Group, "Flying Horse-men," 51

Galdonik, Clair, 90–91
Garcia, Hector, 152, 154–55, 158–61
Garcia, Juan R., 26–27
Garcia, Lupe Picon, 94, 97
Gary, Ind., 42
Gavin, James, 76
G.I. Bill of Rights, 154–55
Gleim, Charles, 58
Godau, Karl, 78
Gold Star Mothers, 10–11, 85, 92
Gomez, Alvina Garza, 122
Gomez, Ambrosia and Amanda, 120, 127
Gomez, Bob, 127
Gomez, Joseph ("Joe"): Army enlistment, 120–22; birth of, 120; combat assign-ments, 128–31; death and burial, 10, 131–32, 140, 145–46; death of mother, 127; growing up in "Little Mexico," 119–20; marriage and children, 122; neighborhood remembrances of, 6; shipment to Korea, 127–28; VFW Post named for, 150
Gomez, Linda Marie, 122, 127, 165
Gomez, Raul ("Buddy"), 120, 127, 131–32
Grant, Madison, 48
Graves Registration Service, 145
Great Depression, The. See Depression of 1929
Grice, Willis, 100
Griffith, D. W., 32
Grottaglie, Italy, 51
Guadalcanal, 5
Guanajuato, Mexico, 24, 28, 47, 84, 93, 134

Hacienda life-style in Mexico, 16–18
Hagerman, Bart, 93, 100, 103
Hanes, Wallace M., 129
Harding, Warren G., 32–33, 40–43
Hayes, William Edward, 43, 137
Heraldo (newspaper), 32–33
Hernandez, Silbiano and Ramona, 16
Herodotus (Greek historian), 158
Hero Street Memorial Park, 159–62, 164
Hero Street war memorial, ii, 164
Herrera, Georgia Sandoval, 63
Herrin, Ill., 40
Hirohito (Japanese emperor), 137

Hitler, Adolph, 117
Hobbs, Leland, 91
Hoover, Herbert, 64, 135
Horn, William F., 41
Huerta, Victoriano, 18–20, 23–24
Hutchinson, Kan., 42

Ibarra, Michael, 150
Ibarra-Gomez VFW Post 8890, 150–51
Illinois Central Railroad, 41
Illinois miners strikes, 40
Illinois National Guard, 5, 41–42
Illinois Western Hospital for the Insane, 30–31
Immigration: forced Mexican repatriation, 39, 46–47; Mexicans as aliens in Amer-ica, 152; post-Revolution immigration, 26–28; pre-Revolution, 7–8; reflecting on the generations, 166; U.S. legisla-tion regulating, 27, 48, 65
India-Burma border, 58–59
International Harvester factory, 110, 137, 153
Irapuato, Mexico, 134–35
Italy, U.S. invasion of, 70–72

Japan: attack on Pearl Harbor, 51; immi-gration to the U.S., 27; invasion of China, 58; surrender, 137
John 15:13 (Bible verse), 133
John Deere factory, 81–82, 85, 153, 161
Johnson, Claudia ("Lady Bird"), 155
Johnson, Lyndon B., 155, 158–59
Joliet, Ill., 42
Jones, J. D., 101

Kennedy, John F., 54
Kennedy, T. W., 154
Kessler, Lloyd L., 61–62
King, Martin Luther, Jr., 148
Klu Klux Klan, 32–33
Korean War: 2nd Street response to, 4–5; Battle of Bloody Ridge, 139–40; Chi-nese entry into, 124–26; combat opera-tions, 123–24, 127–32, 139–40; neighborhood remembrances of, 5–7; North Korean invasion of the South, 122–23, 139; Operation Glory, 145–46; Pusan Perimeter/Inchon Landing, 123; U.S.-Soviet actions leading to, 122
Kuehl, Delbert, 72, 76–77
Kunming, China, 58

La Despolado (Devil's Highway), 27–28
Land ownership in Mexico, 16, 19–20
Ledo Road, 58–59
León, Mexico, 16, 21, 24–25, 47–48, 84, 120
Levino, Frank, 42
Lewis, John L., 40
Lie, Trygue, 122
Little Mexico: 2nd Street name change, 6–7, 158; Billy Goat Hill, 119–20, 132–34; bringing electricity and plumbing to, 57; funeral vigils, 142; Gold Star Mothers, 10–11, 85, 92; Hero Street Memorial Park, 159–62, 164; Hero Street war memorial, ii, 164; paving the streets of, 9, 157–58, 161–62; politics and voter registration, 155–56; post-war employment, 153. *See also* Silvis, Ill.
Little Mexico homes and families: Agapito Masias home, 94, 164; Eduviges Sandoval home, 142–44, 164–65; Gomez family home, 164; Joseph Sandoval (father of Willie) home, 67–68, 164; Joseph Sandoval (son of Eduviges) home, 111; Juan Pompas home, 49, 164; Muños boxcar relocation, 135, 164; Solis family home, 164; Terronez family relocation, 156
Little Mexico rail yard: building a church in, 35–37; closing and relocation, 48–49, 135; immigration to, 7–8; making a home in, 30–33; rail yard dump, 37; Rock Island bankruptcy, 163
Longoria, Beatrice, 154–55
Longoria, Felix, 154–55
Lopez, Al, 149
Lopez, Tony. *See* Pompa, Tony (Tony Lopez)
Lorain, Ohio, 93

MacArthur, Douglas, 123–28
Madero, Francisco, 14, 16–20, 23
Mao Tse-tung, 124
Marshall, George, 124, 127
Masias, Agapito and Epifania (Macias), 93–97, 145
Masias, Johnny, 98
Masias, Lupe, 106
Masias, Mercedes (Macias), 94–97
Masias, Peter (Macias): birth of, 93–94; combat assignments, 99–105; death

and burial, 10, 105–106, 145; drafted into Army, 98; education, 97–98; growing up in "Little Mexico," 94–97; neighborhood remembrances of, 5–6
McCartney, James R., 116–17
McClinton, D. H., 160
McKinley Elementary School, 30, 45, 55, 65, 163–64
McWilliams, Carey, 48
Medals and citations: Frank Sandoval, 63; Joe Gomez, 6, 128, 131; Johnny Muños, 140; Joseph Sandoval, 113, 117; Vicente Ximenes, 158; Willie Sandoval, 74. *See also* Military decorations
Megellas, James, 70, 72–73, 76, 79
Merrill, Frank, 60–62
Mexican Americans: as aliens in America, 152; anti-Mexican sentiments, 32–33; application for citizenship, 156; civil rights movement, 154–56; depression-era employment, 64–65; discrimination toward veterans, 148–51; forced repatriation to Mexico, 39, 46–47, 136; immigration legislation and, 27, 48, 65; patriotism of, 4–5, 8, 10, 153
Mexican-American War, 7, 32
Mexican Revolution: civil war period, 21–26; *Decena Tragicia* (Ten Tragic Days), 20; Díaz ouster, 14–17; mutiny against Madero, 18–19; neighborhood remembrances of, 7; population losses during, 26; U.S. intervention in, 19–20
Mexico: Depression of 1921, 48; Gomez family departure, 120; Muños family departure, 23, 134; Perez family departure, 159; Pompa family departure, 47–48; post-Revolution immigration, 26–28; pre-Revolution immigration, 7–8; Sandoval family departure, 27–30; Silvia Saucedo departure, 22; Solis family departure, 84; Soliz family departure, 23; Terronez family departure, 23
Milan, Ill., 150
Miley, William ("Bud"), 99
Military decorations: Bronze Star, 117; Distinguished Flying Cross, 158; Medal of Honor, 131; Mexican American patriotism and, 153; Presidential Unit Citation, 63, 74, 113; Purple Heart, 63, 113, 117, 128, 140, 146; Silver Star, 6, 131. *See also* Medals and citations

Military units: 38th Regimental Combat Team, 2nd Infantry Division, 139–40; 41st Regiment, 2nd Armored Division, 111–17; 120th Regiment, 30th Infantry Division, 85–91; 132nd Infantry Regiment, Illinois National Guard, 5; 139th Airborne Engineer Battalion, 17th Airborne Division, 98–105; 209th Engineers Combat Battalion, 58–63; 504th Regiment, 82nd Airborne Division, 70–80; 717th Squadron, 449th Bomber Group "Flying Horsemen," 51; 7750 PEC Guard Company, 122; 2nd Armored Division, 105; 38th Infantry Division, 123; Americal Division, 5; "Merrill's Marauders," 60–62. *See also* U.S. Army

Moline, Ill., 9, 159

Moline Dispatch, 158

Moline VFW Post 8890, 150–51, 158, 161, 164

Monroe, Charles, 58, 63

Monterrey, Mexico, 28

Montgomery, Bernard L., 76, 103

Muños, Isabel and Victoria, 134–37, 140

Muños, Johnny: birth of, 135; death and burial, 10, 140; drafted into Army, 139; growing up in "Little Mexico," 133–35; marriage and children, 139; neighborhood remembrances of, 6

Muños, Joseph ("Big Joe"), 23, 134

Muños, Robert ("Big Bob"), 163

Murphy, Vi, 158

Myitkyina, Burma, 59–62

Naples, Italy, 72–73

National Guard, 41–42

National Railway Equipment Company, 163

Nazi Germany, surrender, 10

New Caledonia, 5

New York Times, 32, 42

Normandy invasion, 74–75, 86

North Korea (Korean Democratic People's Republic). *See* Korean War

Nuevo Laredo, Mexico, 28–29, 134

Obregón, Alvaro, 23–24

Operation Cobra, 86–87, 112

Operation Glory, 145–46

Operation Market Garden, 74–80

Operation Varsity, 103–106

Oran, French Morocco, 70

Orozco, Jose Clemente, 23

Our Lady of Guadalupe Church (Silvis, Ill.), 33, 37, 142, 164

Paris, France, 87

Passing of the Great Race, The (Grant), 48

Patriotism: 2nd Street evidence of, 4–5, 10; anti-Mexican sentiments, 32–33; growing up in "Little Mexico," 122; Mexican Americans and, 8, 152–53

Patton, George S., 74–75, 90, 99–102

Paz, Octavio, 7

Pearl Harbor: 2nd Street response to, 4–5, 10; Japanese attack on, 51; railroad response to, 137. *See also* World War II

Peasant/peon class of Mexico, 16–18

Perez, Jesse, 159–61

Pomeroy, Tom, 146

Pompa, Clara, 47, 51–52

Pompa, Dolores, 51–53

Pompa, Frank, 46–47, 49, 52–53, 145, 150, 164

Pompa, Juan and Maria, 46–49, 96

Pompa, Semona, 47

Pompa, Sharon and Tony Jr., 51, 165

Pompa, Tony (Tony Lopez): Army enlistment, 49; birth of, 48; Catholic education of, 45–46; combat assignments, 51–52; death and burial, 10, 52–53, 143, 145; neighborhood remembrances of, 5–6

Pricket, Jack, 90

Racism, KKK and anti-Mexican sentiments, 32–33

Railroads: jobs for Mexican immigrants, 7–8; union strike of 1922, 38–44; WWI nationalization of, 39–40, 46–47. *See also* Chicago, Rock Island and Pacific Railroad; Union Pacific Railroad

Ramirez, Louis, 3–6, 96, 163

Ramirez, Mary Muños, 4, 6, 134–35, 140, 146

Razzo, Danny, 149

Re-internments. *See* Arsenal Island National Military Cemetery

Remer, Ooot-Ernst, 99

Republic of Korea (ROK). *See* Korean War

Reyes, Bernardo, 18

Rhee, Syngman, 122, 124
Rice Funeral Home (Three Rivers, Tex.), 154
Ridgway, Matthew, 71
Rio Grande River, 166
Rivas, Epifania ("Fanny"), 93–94
Rivas, Raymond, 94, 97
Rivas, Tomas, 94
The Rock Island. *See* Chicago, Rock Island and Pacific Railroad
Rock Island Arsenal: Frank Sandoval at, 57; Peter Masias at, 98; post-war employment, 153; Tony Pompa at, 49, 52–53. *See also* Arsenal Island National Military Cemetery
Rome, Italy, 52, 72–73
Romita ("Little Rome"), Mexico, 14–15, 24–25, 28
Roosevelt, Franklin D., 89, 117, 136
Ross, Kirk B., 106
Russia. *See* Soviet Union

Salerno, Italy, 71–72
Saltillo, Mexico, 28
Sandoval, Al, 65–68
Sandoval, Brandon Alfonse, 165
Sandoval, Carmen, 68
Sandoval, Eduviges and Angelina: as aliens in America, 152; burial of Frank and Joseph, 141–43, 150; burial of Santiago, 147; children of, 34; death and burial of, 165; death notices received, 11, 61–63, 113, 117–18, 146–47; Depression of 1929, 43–44, 136; Eduviges as father, 13–14; immigration to the U.S., 27–29; making a home in Silvis, 30–37, 57; marriage, 14–18; railroad strike of 1922, 38–43; religious faith, 14, 20; during the Revolution, 22–23
Sandoval, Emilio, 57
Sandoval, Frank: combat assignment, 60–62; as combat engineer, 57–59; death and burial, 11, 62–63, 113–14, 141–42, 152; drafted into Army, 57; growing up in "Little Mexico," 38, 54–57; naming VFW Post for, 150; neighborhood remembrances of, 5–6
Sandoval, Fred, 65
Sandoval, Harry, 67–68
Sandoval, Henry, 11, 111, 165
Sandoval, Jenny, 28, 39

Sandoval, John, 68
Sandoval, Joseph (father of Willie and Rueben), 64–68, 80, 145, 153
Sandoval, Joseph (son of Eduviges): birth of, 107; combat assignments, 111–17; death and burial, 11, 63, 117–18, 143, 152; drafted into Army, 111; growing up in "Little Mexico," 38, 55, 107–11; marriage and children, 57, 111; naming VFW Post for, 150; neighborhood remembrances of, 5–6
Sandoval, Mercedes, 22, 25, 27
Sandoval, Mike, 11, 111, 165
Sandoval, Nellie, 11, 111
Sandoval, Norberto, 165
Sandoval, Oscar, 80, 145
Sandoval, Pedro, 22, 25, 27–28
Sandoval, Peter, 68
Sandoval, Rueben, 6, 66–68
Sandoval, Rufina, 65–68
Sandoval, Santiago ("Yatch"), 146–47
Sandoval, Tanilo, 12, 22, 28, 43–44, 55, 57, 111, 142–43, 146–47, 149, 165
Sandoval, Willie: Army enlistment, 70; as boxer, 68; combat assignments, 70–79; death and burial, 10, 79–80, 145; neighborhood remembrances of, 5–6; work to support family, 65–68
San Luis Potosi, Mexico, 28
Saucedo, Dolores, 21–22, 25
Saucedo, Silvia, 22
Schools: East Moline High School, 57, 70, 85, 137, 157; McKinley Elementary School, 30, 45, 55, 57, 65, 163–64; St. Mary's school (East Moline), 46, 49
2nd Infantry Division, 139–40
2nd Street. *See* Little Mexico
Segregation. *See* Civil Rights Movement; Discrimination
Segura, Luz, 96–97, 105
717th Squadron/449th Bomber Group "Flying Horsemen," 51
Sierra, Teresa, 35
Silao, Mexico, 28
Silvis, Ill.: anti-Mexican sentiments, 32–33; City Council, 156; civil rights movement, 155–56; closing of the boxcar settlement, 48–49, 135; Gomez family arrival, 120; making a home in "Little Mexico," 30–33; Masias family arrival, 94; McKinley Elementary School, 30,

45; Muños family arrival, 134–35; paving the streets of, 9, 157–58; railroad pedestrian viaduct, 45; Sandoval family arrival, 29–30; Solis family arrival, 84; VFW Post 1933, 148–50, 153, 155. *See also* Little Mexico

Silvis Buffet and Bar, 30

"Sleep, Soldier Boy" (song), 141

Small, Len, 42

Solis, Antonio, 81–82, 84

Solis, Augusto, 84

Solis, Gambino and Manuela, 84

Solis, Joseph Clario: as artist, 81–82; birth of, 84; death and burial, 10, 91–92, 142–43; enlistment in the Army, 85–86; growing up in "Little Mexico," 84–85; neighborhood remembrances of, 5–6

Solis, Kay, 84–85, 92

Soliz, Anthony, 163

Soliz, Chris, 166

Soliz, Clario. *See* Solis, Joseph Clario

Soliz, Frank, 164

Soliz, Guadalupe, 164

Soliz, Joey, 165–66

Soliz, Josie, 23

Soliz, Margarito, 155–56

Soliz, Sonny, 164

Soliz, Tanilo ("Tony"), 139, 164

South Dakota, 51

South Korea (Republic of Korea). *See* Korean War

Soviet Union, 122

Stewart, Carlton E., 115

Stilwell, Joseph, 60

St.-Lô, France, 86

St. Mary of Guadaloupe Church (Romita, Mexico), 14–15

St. Mary's Catholic Church (East Moline, Ill.), 33

St. Mary's Cemetery, 68, 165

St. Mary's school, 46, 49

Suárez, Jose Maria Pino, 19

Sweeney, John, 90

Taft, William Howard, 20

Tapman, Bill, 159

Taylor, Frank, 42

Telegrams, death notification, 9–12

Terronez, Benito and Felisa, 156

Terronez, Jeff, 165

Terronez, Joe: as Frank Sandoval's com-

padre, 54–55; remembrances of, 23, 35, 37; on Silvis City Council, 156–62; as Silvis mayor, 165

Terronez, Tony, 161

38th Regimental Combat Team, 2nd Infantry Division, 139–40

Three Rivers, Tex., 154–55

Time (magazine), 59

Tobias, Thurman H., 62–63

Tomb of the Unknown Soldier, 146

Trujillo, Nick, 156

Truman, Harry S., 117, 122–23

Tucker, Rueben, 71, 76–78

Turner, Damon, 51

209th Engineers Combat Battalion, 58–63

236th Engineers Combat Battalion, 60–61

Unemployment: Depression of 1921, 39, 46–47; Depression of 1929, 136; railroad strikes of 1922, 39–42; union seniority and, 43–44; wartime labor shortages and, 153

Union Pacific Railroad, 163

United Auto Workers (UAW), 157

United Mine Workers (UMW), 40

United Nations (UN). *See* Korean War

Unrecovered remains: Johnny Muños, 146; Willie Sandoval, 145

Uribe, Frances, 94, 97

Urrea, Luis Alberto, 18, 27–28

U.S. Air Force Academy, 165

U.S. Army: body recovery and graves registration, 145–46; death notifications, 9–12, 146–47; Frank Sandoval as draftee, 57; Johnny Muños as draftee, 139; Tony Pompa enlistment, 49; U.S. Eighth Army, 123–24; U.S. Fifth Army, 71–72; U.S. First Army, 86; U.S. Third Army, 74–75, 90, 99; Willie Sandoval enlistment, 70. *See also* Military units

U.S. Army Air Forces: Tony Pompa (Tony Lopez), 51; Vicente Ximenes, 158

U.S. Census, 7, 46–47

U.S. citizenship, 156

U.S. Congressional Record, 5

U.S. Department of Housing and Urban Development, 159

U.S. Deportation Act of 1929, 65

U.S. Equal Employment Opportunity Commission, 159

U.S. Government: denial of veterans bene-

U.S. Government (*cont.*)
    fits, 154–55; immigration restrictions, 39, 47; railroad strikes of 1922 and, 40–43; recognition of Republic of Korea, 122; relations with Mexico, 18–20; War on Poverty, 159; WWI nationalization of railroads, 39–40, 46–47
U.S. Immigration Act of 1917, 27
U.S. Immigration Act of 1924, 48

Vandervoort, Benjamin, 77
Varhola, Michael J., 125, 139
V-E Day (May 8, 1945), 10, 137
Veterans of Foreign Wars (VFW), 148–51, 153, 158, 161, 164
Villa, Pancho, 21–25
Villaseñor, Victor, 21
Visconi, Burt, 96
V-J Day (Aug 15, 1945), 137

Watertown State Hospital, 30–31
Weaver, Robert C., 159
White, Theodore, 59
White supremacy, 32–33
Wilkerson, James H., 43
Willoughby, Charles, 125
Wilson, Henry Lane, 18–20

Wilson, Woodrow, 20, 32, 39–40
Wojciewchoski, L. A., 142
Women: child birth, 35; life in "Little Mexico," 31–33; Mexican Revolution brutality toward, 23; peasant/peon class in Mexico, 16–18; right to vote, 48
World War I: anti-Mexican sentiments, 32–33; nationalization of railroads, 39–40, 46–47
World War II: 2nd Street response to, 4–7; Battle of Bastogne, 89–90, 99–102; Battle of the Bulge, 74, 81, 88–91, 114; body recovery and graves registration, 145; Europe First policy, 59–60; invasion of Italy, 70–74; invasion of Normandy, 74–75, 86; liberation of Paris, 87; Operation Cobra, 86–87, 112; Operation Market Garden, 75–80; Operation Varsity, 103–106; VE Day (May 8, 1945), 10, 117; VJ Day (Aug 15, 1945), 137. *See also* Pearl Harbor
World War II (magazine), 61

Ximenes, Vicente, 158–61

Zapata, Emiliano, 23–24
Zimmerman Telegram of 1917, 32